American Grit

Is It in You?

Confronting Racism, Disenfranchisement, Poverty, and Unemployment

D0062346

NATHANIEL J. FULLER PHD

PAGE PUBLISHING, INC.
New York, NY

First originally published by Page Publishing, Inc. 2018

ISBN 978-1-64138-708-8 (Paperback)
ISBN 978-1-64138-709-5 (Digital)

Printed in the United States of America

Contents

To My Readers

*"**Why this book?**" This book is my Mel Gibson's* Braveheart ***battle cry** to you. See, I love America. America is home to me and my family* (Figure 1). *But America is in big trouble.*

Figure 1. America, my home.

*   **Like** other countries, America is dysfunctional with enduring social issues and problems. **Unlike** other countries, America has **more** to lose if these challenges aren't mitigated. **Why?***

*   As the superpower in the world, America is facing the greatest threats of external and internal terrorism and cyber attacks ever seen in its history. Both external and internal acts of terror and attacks on the Internet are carried out to push racist ideologies. America is **NOT PREPARED** to face these challenges for various reasons, but the **CRITICAL REASON** is because it is plagued with persistent diseases that originated in the homeland around **1472**.*

*   These present-day syndromes are so severe and volatile that I decided to write this book **first** instead of focusing on my nonfiction*

sci-fi thriller **BLACK CYBER**. *No worries though,* **BLACK CYBER** *is being worked, and you will* **LOVE IT**. *For now, buy this book, grab some coffee, and let's begin exploring a* **CURE** *for the enduring diseases of* **racism, disenfranchisement, poverty, and unemployment** *plaguing America.*

Here is our **current** *situation.* Even after the election of the nation's first black president, the *2016 Pew Study: On Views of Race and Inequality, Blacks and Whites Are World Apart,*[1] found profound differences between black and white adults in their views on racial discrimination, barriers to black progress, and the prospects for change.

The study finds the following:

1.   Black and white adults have widely different perceptions about what life is like for blacks in the US. For example, by large margins, blacks are more likely than whites to say black people are treated less fairly in the workplace (a difference of 42 percentage points), when applying for a loan or mortgage (41 points), in dealing with the police (34 points), in the courts (32 points), in stores or restaurants (28 points), and when voting in elections (23 points).

2.   By a margin of at least 20 percentage points, blacks are also more likely than whites to say racial discrimination (70% vs. 36%), lower quality schools (75% vs. 53%), and lack of jobs (66% vs. 45%) are major reasons that blacks may have a harder time getting ahead than whites. More broadly, blacks and whites offer different perspectives of the current state of race relations in the US. White Americans are evenly divided, with 46% saying race relations are generally good and 45% saying they are generally bad. In contrast, by a nearly two-to-one margin,

---

[1].   Pew Research Center, June 27, 2016. "On Views of Race and Inequality, Blacks and Whites Are Worlds Apart."

blacks are more likely to say race relations are bad (61%) rather than good (34%). Blacks are also about twice as likely as whites to say too little attention is paid to race and racial issues in the US these days (58% vs. 27%).

3. About four in ten whites (41%)—compared with 22% of blacks—say there is too much focus on race and racial issues. Blacks and whites also differ in their opinions about the best approach for improving race relations: Among whites, more than twice as many say that to improve race relations, it's more important to focus on what different racial and ethnic groups have in common (57%) as say the focus should be on what makes each group unique (26%). Among blacks, similar shares say the focus should be on commonalities (45%) as say it should be on differences (44%).

MAN, what the hell is going on?!

*Even after the election of the first black president, America seems to be **MORE** divided and cannot **HEAL** or **PROGRESS** from the racial and inequality disease. **WHY?** The answer is straightforward.*

*The sickness of **RACISM and INEQUALITY** has been a part of America's DNA (deoxyribonucleic acid) for "all" my NERD peeps (smile, LOL) since **1472**, and we as Americans **DO NOT** have enough people with **AMERICAN GRIT** to properly confront these issues. What the hell is **AMERICAN GRIT**, you ask? It is the passion and motivation for long-term success for yourself, your family, your colleagues, and America.*

*It is obtained from acquiring **contentment**. **Contentment** is the* state of happiness and satisfaction found through love and respect for oneself and others. Finding ***contentment*** is a challenging journey, especially when faced with continuous adversity like ***racism, disenfranchisement, poverty, and unemployment.***

*This book will provide a pathway for obtaining **your own contentment for your AMERICAN GRIT**. This book is for **everyone and written with love for everyone.***

7

*Why listen to me, you ask? Well, as an **American black man*** (Figure 2) *with meager beginnings, I became a successful avionic technician (AT) for the United States (US) Navy, an **elite** computer scientist for the federal government, and a business entrepreneur. I am **"not"** a celebrity, millionaire, or psychologist who **claims** to have **"all"** the answers to make you successful. **Because I don't.***

Figure 2. Me; everyday American Blackman.

*I do, however, have great experiences as an **"everyday" American black man, son, father, and patriot** that can be used to improve your life and the conditions of your family. I think you can learn from my experiences and recommendations toward achieving **your own happiness**. Before starting, it is important that you understand my background which has influenced my perspective on life.*

*I was born in **great state** of North Carolina (NC) to a loving mother who struggled and is currently struggling with depression. My father was an army veteran, academic, special needs instructor (SEN), and a Baptist minister who devoted his entire life toward understanding the word of God. Together, my parents were a troubled couple who desperately needed separation to become better people toward each other. As a single parent, my father bestowed upon me his views and beliefs on God, while coping with acute diabetes and working various jobs to support us (see figure 3, a picture of my father and I).*

Figure 3. Nathaniel Senior and Junior.

Every morning, we would talk and debate the word of God during breakfast, and we would end our day with thought-provoking discussions on the realities of life and God. Every childhood experience I encountered was coupled to Bible literature and scripture to strengthen my faith and understanding of each event. When I received a poor grade on a test, my father would quote Jeremiah 29:11, "For I know the plans I have for you," declares the LORD, "plans to prosper you and not to harm you, plans to give you hope and a future."

When I got into disagreements and fights with other children, my father would quote Proverbs 16:32, "Better a patient person than a warrior, one with self-control than one who takes a city."

When I felt love for another person, my father would smile and quote 1 Corinthians 13:4–8, "Love is patient and kind; love does not envy or boast; it is not arrogant or rude. It does not insist on its own way; it is not irritable or resentful; it does not rejoice at wrongdoing, but rejoices with the truth. Love bears all things, believes all things, hopes all things, endures all things. Love never ends. As for prophecies, they will pass away; as for tongues, they will cease; as for knowledge, it will pass away."

As I grew into manhood, I would reminisce on all the discussions my father and I had, given that his health and memory were rapidly deteriorating due to his acute diabetes. When I buried my father in February 2010, I was completely at peace because I knew—through his faith and my faith—he was returning to his heavenly home. My mother and I

(Figure 4) *celebrate his existence every time we speak. We look forward to seeing him again. Thank you, Dad, I love you.*
  Okay, let's start.

Figure 4. My mother and I.

Chapter 1

American Grit

The unfair treatment of human beings is *NOT NEW* to America. America has been submersed in **slavery, inequitable civil rights, and racial turmoil** since **1472**, with certain key individuals and groups *OPPOSING* the immoral practices. *GRAB SOME COFFEE, because this short history lesson is important for our discussions in this book.* The following timeline by V. Chapman Smith of UShistory.org[2] provides a summary of the events pertaining to America's *SICKNESS*.

1472
- Portuguese negotiate the first slave trade agreement that also includes gold and ivory. By the end of the 19th Century, because of the slave trade, five times as many Africans (over 11 million) would arrive in the Americas than Europeans.

1503
- Spanish and Portuguese bring African slaves to the Caribbean and Central America to replace Native Americans in the gold mines.

1610
- Henry Hudson's *The Half Moon* arrives in the "New World" mostly likely carrying African slaves. The Dutch were deeply involved in the African slave trade and brought the trade to the American colonies. The Dutch built and grew wealthy on an Atlantic empire of sugar, slaves, and ships.

[2.] Smith, V. Chapman. (2017). *American Anti-Slavery and Civil Rights.* UShistory.org. Available at http://www.ushistory.org/more/timeline.htm.

1619

- A Dutch ship brings the first permanent African settlers to Jamestown, VA.

1641

- Massachusetts becomes the first colony to recognize slavery as a legal institution in 1641 Body of Liberties.

1651

- Rhode Island declares an enslaved person must be freed after 10 years of service.

1663

- A Virginia court decides a child born to an enslaved mother is also a slave.

1671

- George Fox, generally called the founder of the Religious Society of Friends (Quakers), influences agitation among Quakers against slaveholding by Society members when he speaks against slavery on his visit to North America.

1672

- The King of England charters the Royal African Company, thereby encouraging the expansion of the British slave trade.

1676

- Nathaniel Bacon (Bacon's Rebellion) appeals to enslaved blacks to join in his cause.
- Slavery is prohibited in West New Jersey, a Quaker settlement in current-day South New Jersey.

1688

- In Germantown (now Philadelphia, PA), Quakers and Mennonites protest slavery. During this period, these groups worshiped together.

1693

- *An Exhortation & Caution to Friends Concerning the Buying or Keeping of Negroes* by the Philadelphia Monthly Meeting is published in Philadelphia.

1730

- From this time onward, England trades aggressively in North American slaves, with New York, Boston, and Charleston thriving as homeports for slave vessels.

1750

- Georgia is the last of the British North American colonies to legalize slavery.

1754

- John Woolman (b. New Jersey 1720; d. York, England 1772) addresses his fellow Quakers in *Some Consideration of the Keeping of Negroes* and exerts great influence in leading the Society of Friends to recognize the evil of slavery. Philadelphia Yearly Meeting appoints a committee in 1758 to visit those Friends still holding slaves. At the Yearly Meeting in London in 1772, Woolman presents an anti-slavery certificate from Philadelphia. The London Yearly Meeting also issues a statement condemning slavery in its Epistle for the first time in 1754.

1759

- Publication in Germantown (PA) of Anthony Benezet's pamphlet, *Observations on the Enslaving [sic], Importing and Purchasing of Negroes*, the first of many anti-slavery works by the most influential antislavery writer of 18th-century America.

1775

- Founding of the Pennsylvania Society for Promoting the Abolition of Slavery (PAS), the world's first anti-slavery society and the first Quaker anti-slavery society. Benjamin Franklin becomes Honorary President of the Society in 1787.
- Thomas Paine speaks out against slavery and joins the PAS with Benjamin Rush.

1780

- Gradual Emancipation Act passed in Pennsylvania.

1785

- Publication in London of John Marrant's book, *A Narrative of the Lord's Wonderful Dealings with John Marrant, a Black Man*, the first autobiography of a free black.

1786

- Publication in London of *An Essay on the Slavery and Commerce of the Human Species, Particularly the African*, by Thomas Clarkson. Quickly reprinted in the United States, it is the single most influential anti-slavery work of the late 18th century.

1787
- Northwest Ordinance bans slavery in the newly organized territory ceded by Virginia.
- Founding in London of the Society for Effecting the Abolition of the Slave Trade.
- Philadelphia free blacks establish the Free African Society in Philadelphia, the first independent black organization and a mutual aid society.
- The ratified U.S. Constitution allows a male slave to count as three-fifths of a man in determining representation in the House of Representatives. The Constitution sets 1808 as the earliest date for the national government to ban the slave trade.
- Rhode Island outlaws the slave trade.
- William Wilberforce becomes the Parliamentary leader and begins a ten-year campaign to abolish Britain's slave trade.

1788
- Pennsylvania amends law to forbid removal of blacks from the state.

1791
- First American edition of Olaudah Equiano's *Interesting Narrative*, an eye-witness account of the Middle Passage and the first autobiography by an enslaved African, is published in London in 1789.
- Slave insurrection in the French colony of St. Domingue begins the bloody process of founding the nation of Haiti, the first independent black country in the Americas. Refugees flee to America, many coming to Philadelphia, the largest and most cosmopolitan city in America with the largest northern free black community. Philadelphia has many supporters for Toussaint L'Overture.
- Eli Whitney patents the cotton gin, making it possible for the expansion of slavery in the South.

1793
- U.S. Congress enacts first fugitive slave law requiring the return of fugitives.
- Hoping to build sympathy for their citizenship rights, Philadelphia free blacks rally to minister to the sick and maintain order during the yellow fever epidemic. Many blacks fall victim to the disease.

1794

- Founding of the American Convention for Promoting the Abolition of Slavery, a joining several state and regional anti-slavery societies into a national organization to promote abolition. Conference held in Philadelphia.
- The first independent black churches in America (St. Thomas African Episcopal Church and Bethel Church) established in Philadelphia by Absalom Jones and Richard Allen, respectively, as an act of self-determination and a protest against segregation.
- Congress enacts the federal Slave Trade Act of 1794 prohibiting American vessels to transport slaves to any foreign country from outfitting in American ports.

1797

- In the first black initiated petition to Congress, Philadelphia free blacks protest North Carolina laws re-enslaving blacks freed during the Revolution.

1799

- A Frenchman residing in Philadelphia is brought before the Mayor, Chief Justice of Federal Court and the Secretary of State for acquiring 130 French uniforms to send to Toussaint L'Overture.

1800

- Absalom Jones and other Philadelphia blacks petition Congress against the slave trade and against the fugitive slave act of 1793.
- Gabriel, an enslaved Virginia black, attempts to organize a massive slave insurrection.
- Off the coast of Cuba, the U.S. naval vessel *Ganges* captures two American vessels, carrying 134 enslaved Africans, for violating the 1794 Slave Trade Act and brings them to Philadelphia for adjudication in federal court by Judge Richard Peters. Peters turns the custody of the Africans over to the Pennsylvania Abolition Society, which attempts to assimilate the Africans into Pennsylvania using the indenture system with many local Quakers serving as sponsors.

1803

- Benjamin Rush elected president of the Pennsylvania Abolition Society.

1804

- Final defeat of the French in St. Domingue results in the founding of Haiti as an independent black nation, and an inspiration to blacks in America. Haitian Independence Day is celebrated throughout northern free black communities.

1807

- Parliament outlaws British participation in the African Slave Trade.

1808

- United States outlaws American participation in the African Slave Trade. January 1st becomes an instant black American holiday, commemorated with sermons and celebrations. These sermons are the first distinctive and sizable genre of black writing in America.

1813

- Philadelphia black businessman and community leader James Forten publishes his pamphlet, *A Series of Letters by a Man of Color*, to protest a proposed law requiring the registration of blacks coming into the state.

1816

- American Colonization Society is formed to encourage free blacks to settle in Liberia, West Africa.
- Several new independent black denominations are established within the African Methodist Episcopal Church under first bishop Richard Allen.

1819

- Federal law passed requiring the inspection of passenger conditions on ships is used by Quakers to monitor conditions in the slave trade at the Baltimore (Maryland) Port. Society of Friends members accompany federal Customs inspectors.

1820

- Missouri Compromise allows Missouri to become a slave state, establishes Maine as a free state, and bans slavery in the territory west of Missouri.
- The first organized emigration of U.S. blacks back to Africa from New York to Sierra Leone.

1821

- New Jersey Quaker-born Benjamin Lundy establishes the first American anti-slavery newspaper, *The Genius of Universal Emancipation*, in Mt. Pleasant, Ohio. From September 1829 until March 1830, William Lloyd Garrison assists the paper. In 1836–1838 Lundy establishes another anti-slavery weekly in Philadelphia, *The National Enquirer*. This paper becomes *The Pennsylvania Freeman* with John Greenleaf Whittier as one of its later editors.

1822

- Denmark Vesey, a free black, organizes an unsuccessful slave uprising in Charleston, SC.
- Segregated public schools for blacks open in Philadelphia.

1824

- Liberia, on the west coast of Africa, is established by freed American slaves.

1827

- John Russwurm and Samuel Cornish establish the first African American newspaper, *Freedom's Journal*, in New York. The paper circulates in 11 states, the District of Columbia, Haiti, Europe, and Canada.

- Sarah Mapps Douglass, a black educator and contributor to *The Anglo African*, an early black paper, establishes a school for black children in Philadelphia. Mapps becomes an important leader in the Female Anti-Slavery Society and is a life-long friend of Angelina and Sarah Grimke. After the Civil War, she becomes a leader in the Pennsylvania Branch of the American Freedman's Aid Commission, which worked to protect and provide services to the former enslaved in the South.

1829

- David Walker of Boston publishes his fiery denunciation of slavery and racism, *Walker's Appeal in Four Articles*. Walker's *Appeal*, arguably the most radical of all anti-slavery documents, causes a great stir with its call for slaves to revolt against their masters and its protest against colonization.

1830

- Virginia legislature launches an intense debate on abolishing slavery.
- In response to Ohio's "Black Laws" restricting African American freedom, blacks migrate north to establish free black colonies in Canada, which becomes an important refuge for fugitive slaves.
- The first National Negro Convention convenes in Philadelphia.

1831

- William Lloyd Garrison of Boston begins publishing *The Liberator*, the most famous anti-slavery newspaper.
- Nat Turner launches a bloody uprising among enslaved Virginians in Southampton County.

1832

- Maria Stewart of Boston launches a public career as a speaker and pamphleteer. Stewart is one of the first black American female political activists to establish the tradition of political activism and freedom struggle among black women. She calls upon black women to take up what would become pioneering work as teachers, school founders, and education innovators.

1833

- American Anti-slavery Society, led by William Lloyd Garrison, is organized in Philadelphia. For the next three decades, the Society campaigns that slavery is illegal under natural law, and sees the Constitution "a covenant with hell." Within five years, the organization has more than 1,350 chapters and over 250,000 members.

1834

- August 1 becomes another black American and abolitionist holiday when Britain abolishes slavery in its colonies.

1835

- Female anti-slavery societies are organized in Boston and Philadelphia. The Philadelphia Female Anti-Slavery Society was an integrated group of white and black middle-class women, led by Lucretia Mott, Harriett Forten Purvis, and Grace Bustill Douglass. The women met in each other's homes. Bustill, Mapps, and Douglass are prominent black Quaker families in the Philadelphia in the 19th Century.

- Abolitionists launch a campaign flooding Congress with anti-slavery petitions.

1836

- The public careers of Angelina and Sarah Grimke, Quaker abolitionists from a prominent South Carolina family, begin.

1837

- Philadelphia blacks, under the leadership of well-to-do Robert Purvis, organize the Vigilance Committee to aid and assist fugitive slaves. Purvis's wife, Harriett Forten Purvis, the daughter of successful black businessman James Forten, leads the Female Vigilant Society. By his contemporaries, Robert Purvis is referred to as the "President of the Underground Railroad."
- First gathering of the Anti-slavery Convention of American Women, an inter-racial association of various female anti-slavery groups, becomes the first independent women's political organization.
- Founding of the Institute for Colored Youth, which later became Cheyney University, one of the earliest historically black colleges in the United States.

1838

- Philadelphia is plagued with anti-black and anti-abolitionist violence, particularly from Philadelphia white workers who feared that they have to compete with freed slaves for jobs. Second meeting of the Anti-slavery Convention of American Women, gathered in Philadelphia at the newly built Pennsylvania Hall, is attacked by a mob. The mob burns down the hall, as well as sets a shelter for black orphans on fire and damages a black church. Pennsylvania Hall was open only three days when it fell. More than 2,000 people bought "shares" and raised $40,000 to build the Hall. An official report blames abolitionists for the riots, claiming that they incited violence by upsetting the citizens of Philadelphia with their views and for encouraging "race mixing."
- Pennsylvania blacks are disfranchised in the revised state Constitution.
- A Maryland slave named Fred runs away and later becomes Frederick Douglass.

1839

- Abolitionists form the Liberty Party to promote political action against slavery.
- Pope Gregory XVI condemned slavery and the slave trade.

1840

- American Anti-Slavery Society splits over the issue of the public involvement of women. Dissidents opposed to women having a formal role form the American and Foreign Anti-Slavery Society.
- Aged and venerable abolitionist Thomas Clarkson chairs the World Anti-Slavery Convention in London. American attendees include William Lloyd Garrison, Lucretia Mott, and Elizabeth Cady Stanton. American women are not allowed to sit among the men or serve as delegates. On their return to America the women hold a women's rights convention, which met in Seneca Falls, NY, in 1848.
- Martin Delany publishes *The Mystery*, the first black-owned newspaper west of the Alleghenies and he later serves as co-editor of the *Rochester North Star* with Frederick Douglass.

1842

- An angry mob of whites in Philadelphia attacks a black temperance parade celebrating West Indian Emancipation Day. A riot ensues with mayhem lasting three days and resulting in numerous injuries to blacks, who are dragged from their homes and beaten and several homes, an abolitionist meeting place, and a church are set afire.

1845

- *Narrative of the Life of Frederick Douglass, an American Slave* is published in Boston, launching the public career of the most notable black American spokesman of the 19th Century.

1846

- War with Mexico adds significant western territory to the United States and opens a new arena in the fight to check the spread of slavery.

1848

- Free Soil Party is organized to stop the spread of slavery into the Western territories.

- Slavery is abolished in all French territories.
- Women's Rights Convention is held at Seneca Falls.

1849

- Harriet Tubman escapes from slavery. She becomes a major conductor on the Underground Railroad, as well as an advocate for Women's Rights.

1850

- The Compromise of 1850 includes a controversial Fugitive Slave Law that compels all citizens to help in the recovery of fugitive slaves. Free blacks form more Vigilance Committees throughout the North to watch for slave hunters and alert the black community.

1851

- Federal marshals and Maryland slave hunters seek out suspected fugitive slaves in Christiana (Lancaster County), PA. In the ensuing struggle with black and white abolitionists, one of the attackers is killed, another is seriously wounded, and the fugitives all successfully escape. Thirty-six black men and five white men are charged with treason and conspiracy under the federal 1850 Fugitive Slave Law and brought to trial in federal court at Independence Hall in Philadelphia. This trial becomes a *cause celebre* for American abolitionists. Attorney Thaddeus Stevens defends the accused by pleading self-defense. All the defendants are found innocent in a jury trial.

1852

- Congress repeals the Missouri Compromise, opening western territories to slavery and setting the stage for a bloody struggle between pro and anti-slavery forces in Kansas Territory (Bleeding Kansas).

1854

- Lincoln University (Pennsylvania) is chartered in April 1854 as Ashmun Institute. It becomes a higher education institution providing an education in the arts and sciences for male youth of African descent. During the first one hundred years of its existence, Lincoln graduates approximately 20 percent of the black physicians and more than 10 percent of the black attorneys in the United States. Thurgood Marshall and Langston Hughes are among its esteemed alumni.

- Martin Delany leads 145 participants in the 4-day National Emigration Convention in Cleveland, OH. His arguments appeal to some educated and successful northern freed blacks and are defiantly opposite the position held by Frederick Douglass and others. His views represent increasing frustrations in the black community. Six years later, Delany signs a treaty with Nigeria to allow black American settlement and the development of cotton production using free West African workers. However, this project never develops. During the Civil War, Delany works with others to recruit blacks for the 54th Massachusetts and other units. In 1865, Major Delany becomes the first black commissioned as a line field officer in the U.S. Army.

1855
- With the assistance of others, William Still, a leader in the Philadelphia Underground Railroad, and his white colleague Passmore Williamson, intercept slave owner John Weaver, his slave Jane Johnson and her two sons as they are leaving town. The two help Jane and her children leave their master for freedom. Williamson is incarcerated for several months for not bringing Jane Johnson to court. The case becomes a national news story, continuing from August through November.

1856
- The Republican Party, newly formed from various groups opposing the extension of slavery, holds its first convention in Philadelphia.
- Wilberforce University, named English statesman and abolitionist William Wilberforce, opens in Ohio as a private, coeducational institution affiliated with The African Methodist Episcopal Church. This is the first institution of higher education owned and operated by African Americans.

1857
- The Supreme Court's Dred Scott decision declares blacks, free or slave, have no citizenship rights.

1859

- John Brown conducts a raid at Harper's Ferry, Virginia, to free and arm slaves. His effort fails and he is executed.

1861

- Lincoln's election in 1860 leads to Southern states seceding and starts Civil War between the free and the slave states. The Secretary of the Navy authorizes enlistment of contrabands (slaves) taken in Confederate territories.

1862

- First black Union Army forces are organized in South Carolina.
- Charlotte Forten, daughter of Robert Forten and Robert Purvis's niece, heads to Port Royal, South Carolina as teacher for the Philadelphia Port Royal Commission for the "freed" slaves now in Union controlled territory. The *Atlantic Monthly* publishes her essays on her experiences, "Life on the Sea Islands," in 1864.

1863

- Lincoln issues the Emancipation Proclamation abolishing slavery in territory controlled by the Confederate States of America. The Presidential Order also authorizes the mustering of black men as federal regiments.
- The 54th Massachusetts is organized at Camp Meigs, Readville, Massachusetts. Free blacks from throughout the North enlist in the 54th. Other training stations, like Camp William Penn, outside of Philadelphia in Cheltenham are established for training black troops. Between 178,000 and 200,000 black enlisted men and white officers serve under the Bureau of Colored Troops.

1864

- Congress rules that black soldiers must receive equal pay.
- The National Equal Rights League convenes in Syracuse, New York. Delegates are all prominent northern blacks, led by John Mercer Langston who later organized Howard University's Law Department, and included Frederick Douglass and Octavius V. Catto. Working through state chapters, the League promotes an aggressive advocacy agenda to obtain civil rights for blacks. Pennsylvania, New York, Ohio, Illinois, Indiana, and Michigan

are charged to take the lead. Philadelphia blacks, led by Catto, boycott to desegregate public transportation.

1865

- The Civil War ends with a northern victory.
- With their freedom, Southern blacks seek to reunite their families torn apart by slavery, as well as acquire education (particularly reading and writing). Many leave the South for the West and North.
- President Lincoln speaks publicly about extending the franchise to black men, particularly "on the very intelligent, and on those who serve our cause as soldiers."
- Lincoln is assassinated by John Wilkes Booth.
- Andrew Johnson becomes President and begins to implement his own Reconstruction Plan that does not require the franchise for black men in the former Confederate states.
- Many northern states reject referendums to grant black men in their states the franchise.
- Mississippi becomes the first of the former Confederate states to enact laws (Black Codes) severely limiting the rights and liberties of blacks. Other Southern states follow with similar legislation.
- Thirteenth Amendment to the Constitution abolishing slavery is ratified.
- The Freedmen's Bureau is established in the War Department. The Bureau supervises all relief and educational activities relating to refugees and freedmen, including issuing rations, clothing and medicine. The Bureau also assumes custody of confiscated lands or property in the former Confederate States, border states, District of Columbia, and Indian Territory.
- The Ku Klux Klan is formed by ex-Confederates in Pulaski, Tennessee.

1866

- Republicans efforts begin to extend suffrage in the District of Columbia. Initial attempts fail with President Johnson's vetoes. Suffrage is finally granted in 1867.
- Congress passes the first civil rights act. President Johnson's veto of the bill is overturned by a two-thirds majority in both houses

of Congress, and the bill becomes law. Johnson's attitude contributes to the growth of the Radical Republican movement. These Republicans favor increased intervention in the South and more aid to former slaves, and ultimately to Johnson's impeachment.

- Republicans gain veto-proof majorities in both the Senate and the House.
- In Nashville, Tennessee, Fisk University is established for former slaves by the American Missionary Association. The school becomes the first black American college to receive a class "A" rating by the Southern Association of Colleges and Secondary Schools in 1878. W. E. B. DuBois graduates from Fisk in 1888.

1867
- The first election in the District of Columbia to include black voters results in a victory for the Republican ticket. Similar results are repeated in other areas of the country, where blacks are granted the franchise. These elections also produce new black political leaders.
- Congress passes bills granting the franchise to black men in the territories of Nebraska and Colorado, over President Johnson's veto.
- Congress charters Howard University, named after General Oliver O. Howard, Commissioner of the Freeman Bureau and the college's first president. The school's early funding comes from the Freedmen's Bureau. From its outset, it was nonsectarian and open to people of both sexes and all races, although it is considered a historically black college. Howard becomes a premier education institution in the black community and plays an important role in civil rights history. It is here that Thurgood Marshall earns his law degree.

1868
- Fourteenth Amendment is ratified making blacks citizens.
- White voters in Iowa pass a referendum granting the franchise to black voters.
- The Klu Klux Klan evolves into a hooded terrorist organization known to its members as "The Invisible Empire of the South." An early influential Klan "Grand Wizard" is Nathan Bedford Forrest, who was a Confederate general during the Civil War.

1869

- The National Convention of Colored Men meets in Washington, D.C., promoting suffrage for all black men and the education of former slaves. Advocacy and for rights continues through the Equal Rights Leagues. The franchise and other privileges are still denied black men in most northern areas.
- Congress approves an amendment to the Reconstruction bill for Mississippi, Texas, and Virginia, requiring those states to ratify the Fifteenth Amendment before being readmitted to Congress.
- New York becomes the first northern state to ratify the Fifteenth Amendment.
- James Lewis, John Willis Menard, and Pinckney B.S. Pinchback, all black men from Louisiana, are elected to Congress and but are never seated.

1870

- The 15th Amendment is passed permitting black men the right to vote.
- Joseph H. Rainey of South Carolina is the first black to be seated in the House. In all, twenty-two blacks are elected to Congress during Reconstruction. There were seven lawyers, three ministers, one banker, one publisher, two school teachers, and three college presidents.
- Hampton Normal Agricultural Institute is founded by Samuel Chapman Armstrong and chartered as one of the first colleges for blacks. It is also a pioneer in educating American Indians. Booker T. Washington is among its early graduates.
- Pennsylvania, the home of the oldest and largest northern free black community at the time of the Civil War and a major center for the abolition movement, grants the franchise to black men after thirty-two years of disfranchisement.

1871

- National Equal Rights League leader, Octavius V. Catto, is assassinated by a white man attempting to discourage black voting in a key Philadelphia election. Catto's funeral is the largest public funeral in Philadelphia since Lincoln's and his death is mourned in black communities throughout the country.

1875

- The last U.S. Congress of the 19th century with bi-racial Senate and House passes the Civil Rights Act of 1875. The law protects all Americans, regardless of race, in their access to public accommodations and facilities such as restaurants, theaters, trains and other public transportation, and grants the right to serve on juries. However, the law is not enforced, and the Supreme Court declares it unconstitutional in 1883.

1881

- Blanche K. Bruce, Mississippi Republican, ends his term in the U.S. Senate. He is the last black to serve in the Senate until Edward Brooke, Massachusetts Republican, in 1967. With Reconstruction replaced with segregation, voting rights for blacks cease in many areas and greatly curtailed in others.
- Booker T. Washington begins to work at the Tuskegee Institute and builds it into a center of learning and industrial and agricultural training for blacks.

1892

- Ida B. Wells Barnett begins her campaign against the lynching of blacks, a common practice by white racists and the Klan to instill fear in the black community. She later writes *Southern Horrors: Lynch Law in All Its Phases* and becomes a tireless worker for women's suffrage.

1895

- W.E.B. DuBois begins his social analysis of the black conditions in Philadelphia. Published in 1899, *The Philadelphia Negro* becomes a lightning rod for black activism in Philadelphia and other communities around the country.

1896

- Supreme Court establishes "separate but equal" doctrine with Plessy vs. Ferguson. This law enables the expansion of growing segregation or "Jim Crow" practices across America, with many states codifying segregation in state constitutions and local laws and ordinances. By 1910, every state in the former Confederacy fully establishes a system of legalized segregation and disfranchisement. The country largely embraces the notion of white supremacy, which re-enforce the cult of "whiteness" that predated the Civil War. Northern areas also embrace "Jim Crow" practices, some codified in law.

1901

- George Henry White (North Carolina Republican), the last black to serve in the House of Representatives in the 19th Century, leaves office.

1905

- The Niagara Movement, the first significant black organized protest movement of the twentieth century, is launched in Buffalo, NY. It is an attempt by a small yet articulate group of radicals to challenge Booker T. Washington's ideals of accommodation. This militant group was led by W. E. B. DuBois and William M. Trotter.

1909

- A bi-racial group of activists establishes the National Association for the Advancement of Colored People (NAACP) in NYC. The founders, Ida Wells-Barnett, W. E. B. Dubois, Henry Moscowitz, Mary White Ovington, Oswald Garrison Villard (a descendant of William Lloyd Garrison), and William English Walling, make a renewed call for the struggle for civil and political liberty. DuBois becomes editor of the organization's publication, *Crisis* magazine, which presents exposes on conditions and issues in the black community.

1910

- Another bi-racial group of activists establishes the National Urban League to remediate the victimization and deplorable social and economic conditions faced by blacks, who migrated North in hope of better prospects. The organization counsels black migrants from the South, help train black social workers, and works in various other ways to bring educational and employment opportunities to blacks. Its research into the problems blacks faced in employment opportunities, recreation, housing, health and sanitation, and education spurs the League's quick growth with chapters eventually throughout the county.

1914

- Marcus Garvey establishes the Universal Negro Improvement Association, whose motto is "One God, One Aim, One Destiny." The UNIA sets up the Negro Factories Corporation (NFC) to help promote economic self-reliance among blacks. Initially in New York City, UNIA branches are opened in other places, including Philadelphia. In 1935, the UNIA headquarters move to London.

1915

- The release of D. W. Griffith's film, *Birth of a Nation*, which glorifies the Klan and demonizes blacks. The film also inflames race tensions and sets off white attacks on black communities in many areas throughout the United States.

1919

- The Red Summer. Twenty-six documented race riots occur, where black communities across the country are attacked. Hundreds of blacks are killed and even more are injured in these attacks. There is widespread property damage in black neighborhoods. Whites also use lynching as a means to intimidate blacks. In some communities, like the District of Columbia, blacks stand their ground. In the 1920s, riots in Florida and Tulsa destroy the black communities.

1929

- Charles Hamilton Houston, a black graduate of Harvard University Law School, leaves his private law practice to become an associate professor and vice dean of the School of Law at Howard University. In 1932, he becomes dean, a post he holds until 1935. Houston develops an outstanding program in law at Howard, producing many young attorneys who lead the battle to end segregation in public life. Among his students is Thurgood Marshall.
- Oscar DePriest (Illinois Republican) begins term in House of Representatives. He is the last black to serve in the House until the election of William Dawson in 1943.

1936

- Thurgood Marshall leaves private law practice and begins work the National Association for the Advancement of Colored People

(NAACP). He heads the NAACP's Legal Defense efforts and works tireless to end segregation, including the landmark case Brown v. Board in 1954. In 1967, Marshall becomes the first black appointed to the U.S. Supreme Court.

1939

- Billie Holiday records "Strange Fruit"—a haunting song describing lynching. Disturbed by a photograph of a lynching, Abel Meeropol, a Jewish schoolteacher and activist from the Bronx, writes this verse and melody under the pseudonym Lewis Allan. The song increases public recognition of lynching as racist terror. Between 1882 and 1968, mobs lynched 4,743 persons in the United States, over 70 percent of them African Americans.

1946

- President Truman issues Executive Order 9808, establishing the President's Committee on Civil Rights to propose measures to strengthen and protect the civil rights. Truman appoints to the Committee leading black civil rights activist, Sadie Alexander, the first black women to earn a PhD and an early leader in the Philadelphia Urban League. Its report, *To Secure These Rights*, led to Truman's orders to end segregation in the U.S. military and federal Civil Service system. Later in the 1960's President Johnson enlarges Truman's efforts with various civil rights and affirmative action laws to address persistent discrimination.

1954

- Brown v. Board decision declares segregation in public schools illegal.

1955

- The Montgomery Bus Boycott begins on December 5 after Rosa Parks is arrested for refusing to give up her seat to a white man on the bus. This boycott lasts 381 days and ends with the desegregation of the Montgomery, Alabama bus system on December 21, 1956. As a pastor of a Baptist church in Montgomery, Martin Luther King, Jr. leads this black bus boycott and becomes a national hero.

1957

- The Southern Christian Leadership Conference establishes and adopts nonviolent mass action as its cornerstone strategy to gain civil rights and opportunities for blacks. Working initially in the South under the leadership of Martin Luther King, by the mid 1960s King enlarges the organization's focus to address racism in the North.

1959–1963

- King's *Letter from Birmingham Jail* inspires a growing national civil rights movement. In Birmingham, the goal is to end the system of segregation completely in every aspect of public life (stores, no separate bathrooms and drinking fountains, etc.) and in job discrimination. This same year, he delivers his "I Have a Dream" speech on the Washington Mall, which becomes an enduring symbol of King's legacy and influence.

- In Birmingham, a white man is seen placing a box containing a bomb under the steps of the 16th Street Baptist Church, a black congregation. The explosion kills four black girls attending Sunday school. Twenty-three others people are also injured in the blast.

1964

- President Johnson announces the "Great Society" with "abundance and liberty for all," and declares a "War on Poverty." Congress authorizes the Civil Rights Act, the most far-reaching legislation in U.S. history to ensure the right to vote, guarantee access to public accommodations, and the withdrawal of federal funds to any program administered in a discriminatory way.

- Beginning this year, growing frustrations in black communities over urban decay and lack of opportunities erupts into a wave of race riots through U.S. cities, including Los Angeles, Newark (NJ), and Detroit, Michigan. The years 1964 to 1971 see more than 750 riots, killing 228 people and injuring 12,741 others. Additionally, more than 15,000 separate incidents of arson leave many black urban neighborhoods in ruins.

1965

- Voting Rights Act is passed, authorizing direct federal intervention to enable blacks to vote.

- Malcolm X is assassinated by members of the Nation of Islam (Black Muslims) in New York City.

1967

- Robert C. Weaver is appointed Secretary of Housing and Urban Development. He is the first black to hold a Cabinet position in U.S. history.
- Edward Brooke (Massachusetts Republican) becomes the first black to serve in the Senate since Reconstruction.

1968

- On April 4, 1968, James Earl Ray assassinates Martin Luther King, while he is standing on the balcony of the Lorraine Motel in Memphis, Tennessee. In outrage of the murder, many blacks take to the streets in a massive wave of riots across the U.S.
- Congress authorizes the 1968 Civil Rights Act, providing federal enforcement provisions for discrimination in housing. The 1968 expanded on previous acts and prohibited discrimination concerning the sale, rental, and financing of housing based on race, religion, national origin, sex, (and as amended) handicap and family status. This law enabled housing opportunities for blacks beyond the "ghetto."

2008

- On November 4, 2008, Barack Obama is elected President of the United States of America.

2016

- On November 6, 2016, Donald J. Trump is elected President of the United States of America.

Mmmm, interesting American history, right? From the timeline, you see the toxic antiquity of slavery, along with the inhumane deeds and proceedings associated with it. With such a *RICH* history in sadistic behavior, one can clearly see *WHY racism, disenfranchisement, poverty, and unemployment* are *STILL* plaguing *diverse* Americans today in 2018. *If you disagree*, simply revisit the "previous timeline" again, but make sure you have *"stronger coffee"* this time (smile, LOL).

But what you also see from the timeline are the *HEROIC and GALLANT* actions of those *BLACK and WHITE* opposing slavery. Just to clarify, I will repeat. "But what you also see from the timeline are the **HEROIC and GALLANT** actions of those **BLACK and WHITE** opposing slavery."

POP QUIZ! (Already? YUP! [smile]) What was so special about those people and groups, **BLACK and WHITE**, who chose to oppose slavery? Here is my simple answer.

Those people and groups possessed **AMERICAN GRIT**. **GUESS WHAT?** We as Americans today in 2018 need to acquire **AMERICAN GRIT** toward confronting **external and internal threats to America.**

AMERICAN GRIT is the passion and motivation for long-term success for yourself, your family, your colleagues, and America. It is obtained from acquiring **contentment** (figure 5). **Contentment** is the state of happiness and satisfaction found through love and respect for oneself and others **despite** adverse conditions encountered like **racism, disenfranchisement, poverty, and unemployment.**

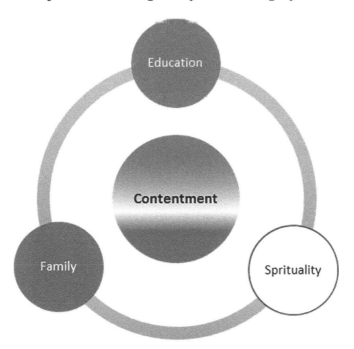

Figure 5. American Grit: Contentment = *education + spirituality + family.*

To achieve *contentment*, one needs *education, spirituality, and family*. These aspects are important to *ALL AMERICANS, but vital* to *high-risk* communities like *American black men, etc. Why?*

American black men are more vulnerable to poverty and unemployment due to *racism, discrimination, and disenfranchisement, according to the 2016 Pew Research Study.*[3] *Education, spirituality, and family* are necessities for American black men toward confronting these issues which directly influence their life expectancy and success. *Education, spirituality, and family* are significant today for black men as they were for African Americans during post-emancipation.

During the post-emancipation era, colleges like Fisk University and Howard University were established to offer African Americans college-level education. Black churches provided communal worship, centers for political organization, and black ministers for community leadership. Black women and men were both homemakers, while collectively contributing to the family income.[4]

Education, spirituality, and family were significant elements in the lives of post-emancipation African Americans. Without these factors, many African Americans would not have made the transition from slavery to freedom. So where does *education, spirituality, and family* measure in the African American community today, specifically with American Black men?

Well, when evaluating *education*, about 48% of black men twenty-five (25) and older attended college, according to 2013 estimates from the US Census Bureau (see figure 6). Half of black men, however, did not complete a degree compared to the 58% of *all men* who attended college. The biggest disparity among black men and *all men* is with those who have a bachelor's degree.

[3.] Pew Research Center, June 27, 2016. "On Views of Race and Inequality, Blacks and Whites Are Worlds Apart."

[4.] Christopher Abernathy et al., "Reconstruction," Nicole Turner, ed., in *The American Yawp*, Joseph Locke and Ben Wright, eds., last modified August 1, 2016, http://www.AmericanYawp.com.

Only 17% of black men have a bachelor's degree compared to the 30% of all men. The number of black men who finished high school but did not pursue higher education is 35% compared to 28% of all men. The percent of black men who have an associate's degree (7%) is equal to that of all men (7%) in America. Only 18% of black men over twenty-five (25) did not complete high school. This is still higher than the percent for men of all races and ethnic groups together.

EDUCATIONAL ATTAINMENT (25 & UP)		
	Black Men	All Men
Less than high school diploma	18%	14%
High school graduate (or GED)	35%	28%
Some college, no degree	24%	21%
Associate's degree	7%	7%
Bachelor's degree or higher	17%	30%
Attended college	48%	58%

Figure 6. 2013 United States (US) Census Bureau Statics on education and American black males.

Based on the previous statistics, education is a **troubled area** for the American black man. **Is there more to this data?** We will explore this topic later in the book. As for **spirituality**, African Americans are more religious on a variety of measures than the US population according to the US Religious Landscape Survey, conducted in 2007 by the Pew Research Center's Forum on Religion and Public Life.

Compared with other racial and ethnic groups, African Americans are among the most likely to report a formal religious affiliation. Eighty-seven percent of African Americans describe themselves as belonging to one religious group listed in figure 7. The Landscape Survey also finds that nearly eight in ten African Americans (79%) say religion is very important in their lives, compared with 56% among all US adults.

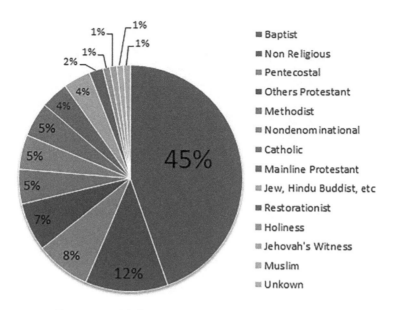

Figure 7. US Census Bureau Statics on common religions for African Americans.

Seventy-two percent of African Americans who are unaffiliated with any faith say religion is an important role in their lives. Nearly half (45%) of unaffiliated African Americans say religion is very important in their lives. More than half of African Americans (53%) report attending religious services at least once a week while more than three in four (76%) say they pray daily.

On each degree, African Americans stand out as the most religiously committed racial or ethnic group in the America. Even those African Americans who are unaffiliated with any religious group pray nearly as often as the overall population of mainline Americans. So there is a resilient relationship between spirituality and the African American community.

Is there a durable relationship between spirituality, gaining education, and a strong family structure? More to come on this topic. As for ***family***, attributes such as marriage has been a declining institution in the black community[5] (see figure 8). Twenty-nine percent of African Americans were married compared to 48% of all Americans in 2014, while 50% of African Americans have never been married compared to 33% of all Americans.[6]

African Americans				All USA
15yrs & older	All	Men	Women	
Married	29%	32%	26%	48%
Divorced	12%	10%	13%	11%
Separated	4%	3%	4%	2%
Widowed	6%	3%	8%	6%
Never married	50%	51%	48%	33%

Figure 8. US Census Bureau Statics on marital status for African Americans.

More black women than black men have been married at least once since more black women are divorced and widowed than black men.[7] The previous statistics suggest that marriage is also a ***troubled area*** for the American black man, right? ***Is there more to the data?*** We will also discuss this later in the book.

*Here are my initial thoughts. When American black men **limit** their exposure to education, spiritual aspects, and family, **contentment** cannot be fully achieved, and **American Grit is diminished**. This condition limits the ability of black men in America to confront **racial discrimination, disenfranchisement, poverty, and unemployment** which contribute to the decline in life expectancy of black men in America.*

*The average African American male lives five years less than the average white American male.[8] The deaths of black men from **police brutality and hate crimes** has prompted national conversation*

---

5. BlackDemoraphics.com (2017). Marriage in Black America. Online: http://blackdemographics.com/households/marriage-in-black-america/.
6. Ibid.
7. Ibid.
8. Lindsey Cook, data editor, "Why Black Americans Die Younger," January 5, 2015.

*about racism, the justice system, policies, and sentencing.[9] **I believe** the implementation of strong family, education, and spiritual awareness are **necessary factors** toward confronting **racial discrimination, disenfranchisement, poverty, and unemployment** that reduce the life expectancy and success of American black men. Meager education, family structure, and spiritual awareness are the key reasons for why the average black baby enters the world under poverty conditions.[10]*

*In 2012, more than two-thirds (2/3) of births in the African American community were to single black mothers.[11] **There is nothing wrong with being a single parent (my father was a single parent).** There is, however, a potential for less wealth and well-being as a single parent since one parent must work harder to elude poverty situations.*

The poverty rate for families with married or stable couples was about 6% in 2013, compared with 30% for families with a single parent.[12] Based on these stats, there is less poverty with married or stable couples compared to single parents. When poverty rates are marginal, parents can provide black babies with a stable environment that fosters positive emotional growth and well-being needed for pursuing college, finding jobs, and partaking in marriage or relationships.

*The life expectancy of an adult American black man is increased when surround by a strong family structure, spiritual awareness, and education leading to healthy income and lifestyle. **So how does one acquire education and strong family structure, while acquiring or sustaining spirituality?** Well, I will provide you with some of **my personal insights and experiences** on achieving these objectives. Let's begin with **education.***

---

9.   Ibid.
10.   Ibid.
11.   Ibid.
12.   Ibid.

Education

Close to half of black men in America are not completing high school or college degrees. There have been several studies and articles that have provided cultural and social reasons for this enduring epidemic. *I will not recap each study or article however, I will survey a few just so we can clearly understand the landscape of the problems.*

One article by Dr. Boyce Watkins titled "Dr. Boyce: Why Aren't Black Men Graduating from College?" provides an overview into the problem. In the article, four (4) factors are discussed:[13]

1. The lack of African American professors in American universities.
2. The lack of value for education by American black men.
3. Meager inner-city school systems and programs.
4. The lack of high expectations within a college or school program.

According to the article, *the lack of African American professors in American universities* causes awkward and traumatic educational experiences for black men because most professors cannot relate to their cultural and social issues. ***American universities are not addressing the problem with hiring qualified black professors.*** The 2013 National Center for Education Statistics report indicates a 43% increase in the award of doctorate degrees to blacks from about 7,000 in 1999–2000 to slightly over 10,000 in 2009–2010; with the average increase in black faculty appointments at a meager 1.3% and the percentage of black faculty at American universities being a humble 4%.[14]

---

13. Dr. Boyce Watkins, "DR. BOYCE: Why Aren't Black Men Graduating from College?"
   https://newsone.com/480662/dr-boyce-why-arent-black-men-graduating-from-college/.

14. 2013 National Center for Education Statistics (NCES): Race/Ethnicity of College and University Faculty and Staff: https://nces.ed.gov/fastfacts/display.asp?id=61.

As for the *lack of value for education by American black men*, the article points out that many black men show more interest in dominating sports (figure 9) rather than academics. The article suggests that more interest in academics should be applied by black men, since the return of investment (ROI) in education is more long term than the profits acquired by professional sports. As for *meager inner-city school systems and programs*, the article notes that inner-city schools are not properly funded relative to suburban schools. Furthermore, black kids are not getting the proper education they need to be successful and America is ignoring the problem.

Figure 9. More interest in dominating sports than academics.

Lastly, *the lack of high expectations within a college or school program* involves black kids going to college expecting to be mediocre rather than exceptional. Many black kids are settling for average performance within the classroom and are not focused on achieving higher academic accomplishment. More focus should be applied to academic excellence instead of social events and parties.

Another study conducted in 2016 by Dr. Shaun R. Harper of the University of Pennsylvania revealed that black men at many mainstream colleges transfer or drop out due to racial pressures, slights, and other negative interactions.[15] More than a hundred and forty (140) students at forty-two (42) predominantly white public and private colleges were surveyed and analyzed. The findings revealed that most high-achieving black male students are victims to racial stereotypes.

Many of the black male students, however, contest racial issues by seeking leadership roles within college organizations (figure 10). Leadership roles are being utilized to change perceptions of black males among their white peers and faculty. Another study by Dr. Derald Wing Sue, a Columbia University psychology and education professor, revealed positive results from social activism and leadership roles, and how these methods give black men a feeling of influence for managing their environments.

Figure 10. Leadership roles.

The study points out that when black men are involved in leadership, it gives them a sense that the locus of control is within

---

15.   Errin Haines Whack, Associated Press. "A new University of Pennsylvania study ties black male college success to campus leadership that can help dispel stereotypes among white peers and faculty," https://www.usnews.com/news/us/articles/2016-02-07/study-explores-how-black-men-find-success-in-college.

them, not others. Furthermore, leadership puts black men in the company of others who are succeeding academically. As black men became more involved on their campuses, their days were more structured, they were more focused, and their grades improved.

Many of the students surveyed got their start as campus leaders through involvement in predominantly black organizations before taking on such roles in more mainstream school groups. This cross exchange of leadership caused students and leaders to confront racial biases so that the responsibility for dispelling myths doesn't fall entirely on black male students.

Other studies such as "Yes, We Can, the Schott Foundation's 50-State Report on Public Education and Black Males"; "A Call for Change," by the Council of the Great City Schools; and "We Dream a World," by the 2025 Campaign for Black Men and Boys, report that black youth are struggling along all points of the academic continuum. Forty-two percent of black students attend schools that are under-resourced and performing poorly. Black boys are three times more likely to be suspended or expelled from school than their white peers, missing valuable learning time in the classroom.

Black and Hispanic males constitute almost 80% of youth in special education programs. Black boys are 2.5 times less likely to be enrolled in gifted and talented programs, even if their prior achievement reflects the ability to succeed. Black male students make up 20% of all students in the United States classified as mentally retarded, although they are only 9% of the student population.

Twenty-eight percent of core academic teachers at high-minority schools lack appropriate certification. Less than half of black male students graduate from high school on time, although many eventually complete a GED. In 2008, 4.6 million black males had attended college, but only half graduated. Nationally, only 11% of black males complete a bachelor's degree.

So now that we have surveyed some of the problems and issues associated with *education*, let's discuss a pathway.

Pathway to Education

As a black child growing up in America, I can certainly relate to the landscape of problems in the previous section. *Many of these problems are systematic and self-inflicted in relation to our meager school systems, and our current values of education to the future of our country. Yet* I am confident that for every problem, there is a solution; and my *Outline to Education* provides a *starting point* and a *baseline foundation* for addressing the problems relative to education. Let's begin by discussing the first step of the outline, which is achieving *Humility Toward Education.*

Humility toward Education

We define *education* as a series of edifying events in which we acquire knowledge toward improving ourselves and the livelihood of our family and community. Your *education* is a personal obligation in which *YOU* are responsible for *NO ONE ELSE. Just to clarify, "your Education is a personal obligation in which YOU are responsible for NO ONE ELSE."*

Your *education* is *ongoing* and can come from a variety of sources such as college courses, books, political groups, the military, social groups, community programs, conferences, music, etc. There is no limit to the sources from which your *education* is derived, and you should seek *every source* for knowledge.

Each source should provide positive information toward *improving yourself, your family, and your community*. For example, opensource.com provides a great list of positive and *free* educational sources: https://opensource.com/education/13/4/guide-open-source-education. For these sources to be beneficial, we must first adopt *humility* toward our educational growth.

Embracing *humility* (figure 11) toward our educational growth involves *accepting the fact* that we have distinct, enduring weaknesses and shortcomings in terms of our knowledge about certain topics and subjects. Now, you are probably thinking, WHAT! SAY THAT AGAIN! I DON'T HAVE WEAKNESSES! *(smile)*. I know, I know; as proud Americans, we tend to see ourselves as *elite* beings with no flaws. ***Conquerors of the universe!***

But trust me, as proud as we may be of ourselves and the accomplishments we have achieved, we have enduring weaknesses and shortcomings in terms of knowledge about certain topics. ***Why?*** Because we are not ***perfect***, and no one has infinite knowledge. ***No one.***

Figure 11. Humility.

So the first step in educating ourselves is ***understanding and accepting*** our distinct, enduring weaknesses and shortcomings in terms of our knowledge on certain topics. I started adopting this concept early in my life. For example,

> *Around the age of five (5) and six (6), I started to realize that my black friends and I spoke differently and used different terms and words differently from my white and Latino class-mates. My black friends and I used both "slang" words and*

English to describe people and certain events; my white classmates used traditional words found in dictionaries exclusively, while my Latino classmates used both Spanish and English. Why was this the case? We were all in the same class, with the same teacher, however, each social group was using words differently, and speaking differently. I did not understand this.

Around the age of seven (7), I would lie down in the backyard of my house and watch the big airliners fly over to land at the local airport behind us. I would wonder how these gigantic machines were able to fly and land so gracefully with great precision. I had no clue about aerodynamics and aviation.

*Around the age of sixteen (16), I fell madly in love **(yeah, madly in love at the age of 16. RIGHT! [smile])** with this beautiful girl. We both really liked each other. Our friends, however, did not approve because I was black and she was white, and made fun of us frequently. Why? This behavior from my so-called friends made no sense to me.*

Around the age of seventeen (17), I started planning for college, however, I had no clue on how I was going to pay for it. I knew nothing about educational loans, grants, and scholarships.

Hopefully you see the pattern here with some of my personal examples. There were a lot of topics like race relations, dating, aviation, and college funding, that I knew nothing about at certain phases of my youth. For me to begin educating myself on these topics, I had to **understand what I didn't know** and **accept the fact that I didn't know about the topic. Once I achieved this state of mind**, it was easy for me to transition into building a **strategy toward educating myself.**

Strategy toward Education

A **strategy toward educating myself** involves creating a plan to achieve your educational goals. The first step of the plan is:

(1) list the ***topics and subjects that you require additional knowledge in*** (figure 12).

Now, this step may be challenging at first because you may not ***know*** what topics and subjects you require additional knowledge in. So to get you started, ask yourself the following question: ***What are my interests, and what activities do I enjoy doing?***

Figure 12. Plan: List your topics/subjects of interest.

As ideas come to your head, simply write them down. *For me, race relations, dating, computers, aviation, and college funding* ***were among the various topics and activities*** *that interested me (Yeah, I know. I'm a nerd at heart [smile]).* I wrote these topics down, along with other topics on my ***whiteboard.*** You can also write and store your topics in a diary, notebook, and ***FREE*** smartphone applications like ***Mindbloom*** (http://www.mindbloom.com) and ***Joe's Goals*** (http://www.joesgoals.com), to name a few.

Just remember, the ***objective*** here is to capture and list all your interests and activities. If you find yourself getting stuck, here are a few recommended topics to get you started:

- ***How to read a book.*** *Reading a book should be a straight-forward task, right? But there are certain techniques that you can use to improve your reading and comprehension* *of the material. This topic is vital for your schooling and employment.*

- **How to negotiate.** *This is a great topic. We all must learn how to bargain to get what we want in life.*
- **Public speaking.** *Also a great topic. We all must have the ability to speak in front of large groups of people.*
- **How to be funny.** *Laughter is a great way to introduce yourself and learn about other people.*
- **How to dress.** *Very important topic. First impressions are crucial when meeting someone who can help you fulfill your goals and dreams.*
- **Exercise and eating good food.** *Having good health is vital toward being successful.*
- **Choosing good friends.** *Having good people around is a critical aspect to your future.*

Hopefully my recommendations were helpful in getting you started with your own lists of topics and subjects. Once your topics and subjects are listed, the next step involves the following:

(2) Ask yourself, *"**Why do I need additional knowledge on these topics and subjects?**"*

The purpose of this question is to really understand your intentions for learning these topics and subjects so that you can **narrow** your list to the ***important topics and subjects. Why is this important?***
I believe that we as human beings spend so much of our valuable time learning about things ***that have nothing to do with improving ourselves, our families, and our communities.*** Most of our learning involves acquiring knowledge about inconsequential interests that gratify short-term and meaningless desires (figure 13). ***Don't get me wrong, there is nothing wrong in learning fun and stress-free topics/subjects in moderation (keywords, "in moderation").***

Figure 13. Wasting time.

But sometimes we *"go overboard"* in learning things that have no benefit to our growth. *For example, there were plenty of nights where I decided that "mastering Super Mario Brothers while listening to The Cure" was vital to my existence. Also, "playing POKER until 3 AM" on a school night seemed to be a reasonable and responsible thing to do (especially after a few drinks [smile]).*

*The reality is, "playing Super Mario Brothers and POKER" did not improve me, my family, or my community. I have not become a BIG Nintendo executive or a RICH casino owner from playing Super Mario Brothers and POKER. I HAD A LOT OF FUN DOING IT (smile), but I gained **nothing** from these activities toward improving myself, my family, and my community.*

So **stay away** from topics, subjects, and interests that do not **directly improve** yourself, your family, and your community. **Don't waste your valuable time** learning about topics and subjects that do not contribute to your **direct** success and the success of your family and community. **Invest your time** in worthwhile subjects that are directly tied to your success.

Upon accomplishing this task, you can proceed to the next step:

(3) Get additional knowledge about your topics/subjects.

This step can also be "tricky" because you may not know how and where to go to get information about topics/subjects of interest.

I have one word for you: **TECHNOLOGY**. *Now, I know that is a simple geek answer.*

But technologies like *YouTube* and *GOOGLE* search engines (figure 14) are somewhat assessable to everyone today *via your smartphone*, thus, we need to use this type of technology for educating ourselves on *positive topics/subjects* for *improving ourselves, our families, and our communities*.

Figure 14. Technology: Search engines.

Media Smarts at http://mediasmarts.ca/tipsheet/how-search-internet-effectively provides the following instructions on how to search the Internet effectively for topics/subjects:

- Ask your question the right way so that you don't end up overwhelmed with too many search results, underwhelmed with too few, or simply unable to locate the material that you need.
- Before doing an Internet search, it's important to define your topic as completely and succinctly as possible. Write down exactly what information you're looking for, why you're looking for it, and what you're not looking for. This will help you to discover the best keywords for your search.

- Search engines don't read sentences the way people do: instead, they look for the key words in your query in the websites they search. In other words, you're not asking a search engine a question, you're asking it to look for websites where those words appear. To use a search engine or database effectively, therefore, you need to be able to choose the best combination of key words.
- Most search engines work best if you provide them with several keywords. So how do you determine which keywords will work best?
- Think about what you're searching to determine the essential key words. For instance, if you're just looking for a recipe for peanut butter cookies, you can write peanut butter cookie recipe. But if you're looking for a recipe that doesn't use flour, you can write peanut butter cookie recipe flourless (the order of the words doesn't matter) and if you want a flourless recipe that uses natural peanut butter you can write peanut butter cookie recipe flourless natural.
- Now you have your keywords. How do you enter them into the search engine? Your most powerful keyword combination is the phrase. Phrases are combinations of two or more words that must be found in the documents you're searching for in the EXACT order shown. You enter a phrase—such as "peanut butter"—into a search engine, within quotation marks. Most search engines allow you to use quotation marks or square brackets to do a phrase search as in "peanut butter" or [peanut butter].
- If you find that you're getting results that aren't what you're looking for, you can use a minus sign to exclude results that include a certain word or phrase. So, if you want recipes that use peanut butter but aren't cookie recipes, you could use "peanut butter" recipe –cookie (the minus sign must be directly before the word you want excluded, with no space in between). You can also limit your search by type, time or country. Most search engines

have tabs at the top that let you choose between websites, images, videos, news stories, and so on. Many also have advanced search tools that let you limit your search to just one country, a certain time (the last day, week, month, year, or a range you specify).

- If there's a site that you know is reliable, most search engines will let you limit your search to just them. Just add the web address at the end of your search string, like this: peanut butter cookie recipe flourless natural site: www. epicurious.com. (Make sure not to put a space between site: and the web address.)

The previous instructions by Media Smarts are excellent guidelines for searching the Internet effectively for **instructional and positive** topics/subjects. As mentioned previously, we need to **cease** in using technology toward attaining intelligence on **frivolous** interests. As a young black male, I sought out technologies like **cable television** for educating myself on **race and culture** and **dial-up Internet (Yeah, dial-up Internet connection [laugh])** toward educating myself on **college funding options.**

*For example, Music Television (MTV), which was launched on August 1, 1981, introduced me to diverse personalities that shaped my perspective on **culture and race relations**.*

It exposed me to various artists who were expanding their outreach to their own race and other races. Michael Jackson, Prince, Eddy Grant, Donna Summer, Musical Youth, David Bowie, Tina Turner, and Herbie Hancock were among the first MTV artists who influenced me with their diversity.

MTV bands like The Specials, Big Country, Fine Young Cannibals, Simple Minds, and The Power Station had integrated lineups of white and black musicians and vocalists, which shaped my vision on racial and cultural integration. Chuck D and Public Enemy, who made an appearance on Yo! MTV Raps *in 1988, were crucial toward shaping my sentiments for myself as a black male and for other black men that I knew. Their music introduced me to the violent and* *tragic history of **racism and discrimination** not only in America, but in the world.*

*Around 1989, I used dial-up Internet services like AOL to search and collect information on colleges and funding options for paying college tuition. This technology allowed me to gain valuable information about grants, financial aid, work-study programs, and scholarships. I collected this information and presented to my father and my high school advisor so that we could **collectively** build a plan for paying for my college education.*

I hope you see the pattern here with some of my personal examples in using **technology**. During my adolescent phase, I used current technology for educating myself on **relevant** information, **not inconsequential** material. I did not **waste my time** in attaining intelligence on **frivolous** subjects, and **neither should you**. This will only **delay** you from going to step four (4) which is,

(4) Execute training.

This step involves executing training toward **mastering** your topics, subjects, and interests. Your training is **ongoing** and can come from a variety of sources such as college courses, books, political groups, the military, social groups, community programs, conferences, music, etc. *My training involved going to college (figure 15) and joining the military (figure 16, GO, NAVY!).*

*I had several reasons for my training choices. First, getting a college education **is vital for "all" Americans and extremely vital for American black men** like myself who are more vulnerable to poverty and unemployment due to **racism, discrimination, and disenfranchisement**. For me to confront these toxic social conditions plaguing our country, I needed to equip myself with the **"necessary tools."** A college degree is a **"necessary tool."***

*Second, **my love for country** and my interest in aviation influenced my decision to join the military. Joining the US Navy gave me the opportunity to earn money for college and for my family, while serving*

my country and working on aviation aircraft. My experience in the US Navy was one of the most indispensable periods in my life.

Figure 15. Doctorate degree presentation.

Figure 16. Avionic technician (AT) Nathaniel J. Fuller.

By far, the training phase is the ***hardest step*** of your educational journey because it requires you to have ***discipline, dedication, and tolerance*** during periods of adversity. *During my college journey, I had to apply a great amount of **focus and restraint** given that I was faced with*

*several challenges such as **my father passing away, relationship separa-***
***tion, getting married, having children, and working full-time**. I*
*also faced more complex problems such as **racism and discrimination***
while in college, the military, and in the federal government.

*****Racism and discrimination** are enduring issues in America (figures*
17, 18, 19), and confronting these issues required me to constantly evaluate
*my **discipline, dedication, and tolerance** toward **my beliefs in diver-***
***sity for achieving my educational goals**. As I interacted with differ-*
ent people in college, the military, and the federal government, it became
apparent that various people and groups of people had different viewpoints
on race relations. Many people and groups that I met were not interested in
*race and cultural integration and preferred to live and work in **separation**.*

Figure 17. The Selma to Montgomery marches held in 1965
from Selma, Alabama, to the state capital of Montgomery. The
marches were organized by nonviolent activists to demonstrate the
desire of African-American citizens to exercise their constitutional
right to vote, in defiance of segregationist repression.[16]

---

16. Sheila Jackson Hardy, P. Stephen Hardy (August 11, 2008). *Extraordinary People of the Civil Rights Movement*. Paw Prints. p. 264. ISBN 978-1-4395-2357-5. Retrieved March 6, 2011.

Figure 18. The Edmund Pettus Bridge in Selma became a Civil Rights Movement landmark when, on March 7, 1965, 525 civil rights marchers on their way to march from Selma to Montgomery attempted to cross the bridge, but were turned back and attacked by Alabama state troopers and members of the Ku Klux Klan (KKK).[17]

---

17. *United States Congress.* "PETTUS, Edmund Winston (id: P000279). "*Biographical Directory of the United States Congress.*

Figure 19. By refusing to give up her seat to a white man on a Montgomery, Alabama, city bus in 1955, black seamstress Rosa Parks (1913–2005) helped initiate the civil rights movement in the United States.[18]

*To put it simply, many of these people and groups preferred to be racist and used racism as a tool for **division** in our learning environments and workspaces. Now, there are various studies that have been done on how racism and discrimination is detrimental to our country. I will not recap these studies for this book, however, what I will say as a former government representative is this: **"Racism and discrimination are national security threats for America."***

---

18. Juan González, Amy Goodman (March 29, 2013). "The Other Rosa Parks: Now 73, Claudette Colvin Was First to Refuse Giving Up Seat on Montgomery Bus." *Democracy Now!* Pacifica Radio. 25 minutes in. NPR. Retrieved April 18, 2013.

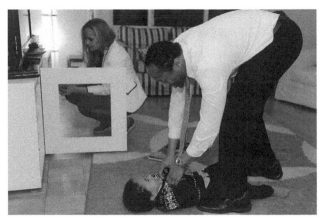

Figure 20. Live every day like it is your last.

There is no cost-effective method for us as Americans to confront **external and internal terrorism and cyber attacks** *with racism and discrimination* **embedded into our way of life.** *The existence of bigotry and prejudice in our way of life* **only** *fuels the hatred and loathing that breeds terrorism and attacks on the country and on the Internet. Furthermore, these threats are and will have greater impact on* **"everyday people,"** *the poor, and the less educated,* **both white and black.**

Thus, it is vital for **high-risk communities** *like* **American black men and others** *to have* **continence, commitment, and forbearance** *toward racism and discrimination when fulfilling educational training for improving oneself. This concept worked for me, and it can certainly work for you. Here are my recommendations for doing this:*

1. ***Understand your value.*** *No one controls or determines your value to the world but you. Once you understand and accept your importance, focus all your efforts on preserving and refining the aspects of your life that directly advances yourself, your family, and your community.*

2. ***Live every day like it is your last*** *(figure 20). When you adopt this mind-set, I mean* **truly** *accept the fact that your life is not guaranteed every day, you become conditioned in appreciating the important aspects of your life, e.g., love, your*

family, your legacy to your family and friends, etc. Try to realign your thinking toward valuing the essential facets of your existence.

3. ***Embrace and learn from failure.*** *When trying to succeed, no matter the undertaking, you will experience **failure**. Embrace it, then learn from it. You don't have to like failing, but you need to know how to deal with it in a manner that spawns **positivity** after a failure.*

4. ***Learn from everyone, listen to a few.*** *Understand that it is perfectly acceptable to **learn** from everyone you meet and interact with. It is not acceptable to **listen** to everyone since people have different motives that may not include your **best** interests. Thus, you must be selective toward advice and suggestions offered.*

5. ***Pass along your knowledge to others.*** *The best part about improving yourself through training is passing your "newly" acquired knowledge on to others who desire it. Your educational journey is not only about improving yourself; it is also about improving your family and your community.*

So *ARE YOU STILL WITH ME? GREAT!* Let's recap this section before moving into ***family***. *Initially*, we must first adopt **humility** toward our educational growth. *Then, we need a **strategy** toward educating ourselves.* This involves creating a plan to achieve your educational goals. The steps of the plan are as follows:

1. ***List the topics and subjects that you require additional knowledge in.***

2. ***Ask yourself, "Why do I need additional knowledge on these topics and subjects?"***

3. ***Get additional knowledge about your topics/subjects.***

4. ***Execute training.***

*Good? Now, let's talk about **family**.*

Chapter 2

Family

As mentioned earlier in this book, family attributes such as marriage (figure 21) has been a declining institution in the black community.[19] Twenty-nine percent of African Americans were married compared to 48% of all Americans in 2014, while 50% of African Americans have never been married compared to 33% of all Americans.[20] More black women than black men have been married at least once since more black women are divorced and widowed than black men.[21]

Figure 21. Marriage.

19. BlackDemoraphics.com (2017). Marriage in Black America. Online: http://blackdemographics.com/households/marriage-in-black-america/.
20. Ibid.
21. Ibid.

So what is going on in the black community in terms of marriage, specifically with American black men? Here is my answer. Like other men, not all American black men are interested in getting married, but the ones that are interested are *delaying or separating from* the idea of marriage because they see it as a milestone that can only be considered upon gaining *(1) wealth or prosperity, and (2) satisfying personal desires*. Let's talk about *wealth* first.

Wealth/Prosperity

Most American black men are *delaying or separating from the idea of* marriage until a *certain level of income* is obtained. *Why?* Because American black men *are still twice as likely to live in poverty or be unemployed*, according to the highly regarded *2016 Pew Research Study*.[22]

According to the 2016 Pew study, the modern black man is still more vulnerable to poverty and unemployment due to discrimination and disenfranchisement.[23] *To avoid poverty and unemployment, it is my belief that American black men choose to focus their time and efforts on seeking legitimate job opportunities leading to significant money, instead of marriage. My father (Figure 22) is a good example of my theory.*

---

[22] Pew Research Center, June 27, 2016. "On Views of Race and Inequality, Blacks and Whites Are Worlds Apart."

[23] Ibid.

Figure 22. My Father.

When my father and mother separated/divorced, my father had no interest in rekindling his marriage to my mother or remarrying given that his focus was primarily on making money toward rising me. My father was an ordained minister and an army veteran with advanced degrees in education, however, he had difficulties finding stable work with a reasonable salary. Thus, my father worked various low-income jobs to support us. When I graduated high school and left for college, my father decided to reduce his workload given that his expenses were lowered since I was in college and on my own. My father dated from time to time, but he never remarried.

So although my father had been previously married, when separated/divorced, he chose to focus his attention on obtaining money and wealth toward rising me instead of marriage.

Another good example to my notion are the survey responses from a 2010 article by *Donna Britt titled "Why Do Black Men Have an Aversion to Marriage?"* In the article, seven single, never-married, childless black men over thirty (30) were surveyed on their singleness. Various responses to the survey questions were received, with some of the ***pertinent responses below*** relating to obtaining financial stability.

- ***Washington, D.C. high school teacher, 36:*** *"It ain't a love thing, it's a bill thing . . . a question of economics. Not having the stable, corporate job creates pressure. I want a certain* *amount of stability before marriage, and a lot of black men feel unstable financially."*

- **Washington, D.C., area businessman, 37:** *"Personally, I focus most of my attention on business. And have always put before my challenges that warrant most of my energy, time and thought. Developing a relationship requires the same. And I haven't been that motivated."*

The previous responses to the survey questions reflect direct interest in obtaining financial stability before considering **marriage**. **My notion** has also been proven by researchers like Oppenheimer (1988),[24] Edin (2000),[25] Lawson and Thompson (1999),[26] Schneider (2011)[27], and Goldscheider and Waite (1986)[28] where their findings reflect a strong relationship between **marital formation** and **job security**.

- Amongst **all** men, career decisions will impact marital aspirations; deciding to marry early may negatively impact a man's ability to experiment with different jobs in search of more fulfilling work (Oppenheimer, 1988).[29]

- Men will also **delay or separate from the idea of** marriage until they achieve specific milestones inclusive of working a steady job, owning a car or a boat (Figure 23), residing

24. V. K. Oppenheimer (1988). A theory of marriage timing. The American Journal of Sociology, 94 (3), 563–591.
25. K. Edin (2000). What do low-income single mothers say about marriage? Social Problems, 47(1), 112–133. doi: 10.1525/sp.2000.47.1.03x0282v.
26. E. J. Lawson and A. Thompson (1999). Black men and divorce. Thousand Oaks, CA: Sage Publications.
27. D. Schneider (2011). Wealth and the marital divide. American Journal of Sociology, 117 (2), 627–667.
28. F. K. Goldscheider, and L. J. Waite (1986). Sex differences in the entry into marriage. American Journal of Sociology, 92 (1), 91–109.
29. V. K. Oppenheimer (1988). A theory of marriage timing. The American Journal of Sociology, 94 (3), 563–591.

in a home, and securing financial assets (e.g., bank account, retirement account) (Edin, 2000;[30] Lawson and Thompson, 1999;[31] Schneider, 2011[32]).

- Postponing marriage is particularly likely for men who have not yet achieved these milestones (Goldscheider and Waite, 1986;[33] Schneider, 2011[34]).

Figure 23. Owning assets, like a car or boat.

Based on the previous data, *my notion* of American black men *delaying or separating from* the idea of marriage until *wealth* is obtained is somewhat valid, right? *Who wants to enter a marriage in poverty and unemployment?* So to improve marriage rates for Black men, we need to focus *only on* improving their job opportunities, correct? What about satisfying *personal desires* before marriage? Let's discuss this further.

[30] K. Edin, K. (2000). What do low-income single mothers say about marriage? Social Problems, 47(1), 112–133. doi: 10.1525/sp.2000.47.1.03x0282v.

[31] E. J. Lawson, and A. Thompson (1999). Black men and divorce. Thousand Oaks, CA: Sage Publications.

[32] D. Schneider, D. (2011). Wealth and the marital divide. American Journal of Sociology, 117 (2), 627–667.

[33] F. K. Goldscheider, and L. J. Waite (1986). Sex differences in the entry into marriage. American Journal of Sociology, 92 (1), 91–109.

[34] D. Schneider (2011). Wealth and the marital divide. American Journal of Sociology, 117 (2), 627–667.

Personal Desires and Preferences

American black men have various desires and preferences on marriage and relationships given that *each black man is different* (figure 24). Despite erroneous *misconceptions and racial stereotypes, all* black men are not the same and do not share the same desires and preferences. *I will repeat, just to clarity. All* black men are not the same and do not share the same desires and preferences.

Figure 24. Diverse black men.

Thus, *racial stereotyping and generalizing* black men collectively as a group is *simply fatuous* from a statistical perspective. Each black man is different and has distinct personal preferences and desires that influence their decisions on relationships, marriage, and family. Again, the survey responses from *Donna Britt's article titled "Why Do Black Men Have an Aversion to Marriage?" provides a qualitative example to my notion*.

As mentioned previously, seven single, never-married, childless black men over thirty (30) were surveyed on their singleness. The various responses *below* were obtained, reflecting *different personal desires and preferences* about marriage.

- *Washington, D.C., area media professional, 34: "I want marriage. But part of me doesn't—it's the part that thinks that the moment I settle down, the real one will come along, and I'll say, 'Damn it, I settled on this one.' . . . The other [thing] is that your ego gets so much gratification from so* many women being around. And even if you get one you like, you're reluctant to give up . . . the thrill of dealing with different ones, new one . . . . And I really want to be faithful once I make that promise."

- **Los Angeles musician, 35:** "As shallow as it sounds, if I got married, I would miss the exhilaration of a new relationship. I would feel guilty saying I would forsake all others, knowing that I'm a good candidate for fooling around. I don't while I'm in relationships, but I see them . . . as lasting for two or three years at most. So, I can afford to be faithful. The one time I was in a relationship that looked like it might lead to marriage, I was the horniest I've ever been. . . . Does that make sense? Frankly, when you're switching women, you don't have to confront your own mortality. I'm dating a 23-year-old, therefore I'm still young and with it."

- **Detroit physician, 36:** "Once, the availability of women was an influencing factor. But my sex life is damn dry now, has been for a while. But just as women's marriage hopes spring eternal, for men, there's the specter . . . that just around the corner, a new sexual adventure awaits. . . . For me, marriage feels like a loss of freedom . . . entrapment. And I don't want children, so what does marriage hold? But I am starting to see some advantages—primarily that I won't be able to pull off this lifestyle forever. And I think that it has become very acceptable for black men not to marry, just like it is for some black women to have children out of wedlock. . . . Another thing that may play into it is the importance in the black male subculture of being sexually potent. . . maybe because we have so little status elsewhere."

- **Washington, D.C., professional writer, 35:** "Right now, I'm trying to juggle two women. If I were a good enough liar, it could be three . . . four or five. In cities like Washington, it's like Fantasy Island. . . . But I absolutely want to marry. I *grew up in a Donna Reed household, and I want a family. So much of the pool of eligible black men is in jail or dead. . . . But the critical thing is that too many black men do not see their lives being enhanced by marriage. . . . They don't understand that you amass more money, your kids get a healthier life . . . the whole picture. All my friends who got married early, their lives seem fuller. And you know how people visualize having someone to grow old with? Black men don't grow old, so what's the point? By the time we get to 25, we feel we're half done anyway. 'On Golden Pond'—you don't see Billy Dee Williams in that."*

- ***Dallas health club supervisor, 32:*** *"If I can cook, clean, sew on a button . . . my woman should be able to, too. When my father died, my mother was able to take over. We all went to college. . . . I want that strength. Years ago, when I had what I wanted, I blew it. Now the woman I'm looking for, I can't find."*

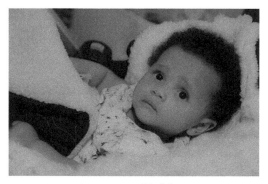

Figure 25. Children.

Based on the various responses above, it is **very clear** that American black men are different from one another and have **different personal preferences and desires** that influence their decisions on relationships, marriage, and family. Some black men are **simply not ready** for marriage due to **various desires and preferences** such as dating numerous people, or not wanting to have children (Figure

25), or they haven't found the right one yet—*the list can go on and on*. So if each American black man is different from one another, and has *distinct personal preferences and desires* that influence his decisions on relationships, marriage, and family, *why do we (Americans, media, etc.) continue to racially stereotype and generalize black men collectively as a whole?*

Here is my simple answer. Americans *(blacks, whites, Latinos, Indians, etc.) continue to racially stereotype and generalize* black men collectively because it simplifies *our* world and reduces the amount of *thinking* needed when confronting black men,[35] or confronting social issues that impact black men. By stereotyping, we infer that *all* black men have the same assumed characteristics and abilities, which leads to *prejudice attitudes and negative impressions.*[36]

It is also *my belief* that *racial stereotypes and generalizations* influence the *desires and preferences* of American black men. Research conducted by Steele and Aronson (1995)[37] and Shih, Pittinsky, and Ambady (1999)[38] concur with *my theory*. Steele and Aronson (1995) conducted an experiment involving African American and white college students who took a difficult test using items from an aptitude test (American GRE verbal exam) under one of two conditions.

In the stereotype threat condition, students were told that their performance on the test would be a good indicator of their underlying intellectual abilities. In the non-threat condition, students were told that the test was simply a problem-solving exercise and

---

35. S. A. McLeod (2015). Stereotypes. Retrieved from www.simplypsychology. org/katz-braly.html.

36. Ibid.

37. C. M. Steele, and J. Aronson (1995). Stereotype threat and the intellectual test performance of African Americans. *Journal of personality and social psychology, 69(5)*, 797.

38. M. Shih, T. L. Pittinsky, and N. Ambady (1999). Stereotype susceptibility: Identity salience and shifts in quantitative performance. *Psychological science, 10(1)*, 80–83.

was not diagnostic of ability. Performance was compared in the two conditions, and results showed that African American participants performed less well than their white counterparts in the stereotype threat condition.

In the non-threat condition, their performance equaled that of their white counterparts. In another study conducted by Shih, Pittinsky, and Ambady (1999), Asian women were subtly reminded (with a questionnaire) of either their Asian identity or their female identity prior to taking a difficult math test. Results showed that women reminded of their 'Asianness' performed better than the control group. Women reminded of their female identity performed worse than the control group.

According to Steele, stereotype threat generates *"spotlight anxiety"* (Steele and Aronson, 1995, p. 809), which causes emotional distress and "vigilant worry" that may undermine performance. Students worry that their future may be compromised by society's perception and treatment of their group so they do not focus their full attention on the test questions. Students taking the test under stereotype threat might also become inefficient on the test by rereading the questions and the answer choices, as well as rechecking their answers, more than when not under stereotype threat. It also can induce "attributional ambiguity"—a person gets a low grade and asks, *"Is it something about me or because of my race?"*

I believe that racial stereotypes and generalizations about American black men generate *spotlight anxiety*[39] that causes black men to believe that their future is *already* compromised by society's perception (figure 26). I believe that *spotlight anxiety* [40] influences the *desires and preferences* of American black men toward marriage, relationships, family, etc. *(the list can go on and on)*. Furthermore, this anxiety causes American black men to induce

---

[39]. C. M. Steele, and J. Aronson (1995). Stereotype threat and the intellectual test performance of African Americans. *Journal of personality and social psychology, 69(5)*, 797.

[40]. Ibid.

"attributional ambiguity" toward marriage, relationships, family, etc. *(the list can go on and on).* As a result, black men have the sense of, "*Well, since I am black, I am faced with racial discrimination, poverty, and unemployment, **thus,** marriage, family, etc., is not my primary focus right now. I need to focus on my survival for dealing with these issues [wealth, businesses, not getting married, not being a responsible parent, seeking wealthy partners, crime, selling drugs, etc., the list can go on, and on].*"

Figure 26. Spotlight anxiety.

So if you are still with me, great! (Smile.) Let's recap this section before moving into my guidance.

1. ***Not all*** American black men are interested in getting married, but the ones that are interested are ***delaying or separating from*** the idea of marriage because they see it as a milestone that can only be considered upon gaining *(1) **wealth or prosperity, and (2) satisfying personal desires**.*

2. In terms of ***wealth***, most American black men are ***not interested*** in marriage until a ***certain level of income*** is obtained. ***Why?*** Because American black men ***are still twice as likely to live in poverty or be unemployed***,

according to the highly regarded *2016 Pew Research Study*.[41]

3. American black men have various desires and preferences on marriage and relationships given that *each black man is different from one another*. Despite erroneous *misconceptions and racial stereotypes*, *all* black men are not the same and do not share the same desires and preferences.

4. *I believe that racial stereotypes and generalizations* about American black men generate *spotlight anxiety*[42] that causes black men to worry that their future is *already* compromised by society's perception (Figure 26). I believe that *spotlight anxiety*[43] influences the *desires and preferences* of American black men toward marriage, relationships, family, etc. *(the list can go on and on).*

With all these issues to confront, how does one acquire strong family structure? Let's talk about a *pathway.*

Pathway to Strong Family Structure

Foremost, I believe that **marriage** *(figure 27) is the critical attribute to a strong family structure.* There have been various studies, articles, and documentaries on how important *marriage* is toward achieving this goal. One study by Dr. Tera R. Hurt titled "Black Men and the Decision to Marry,"[44] tries to understand the decision to marry among a sample of fifty-two (52) married black men. Qualitative inquiry was used to explore this issue.

---

41. Pew Research Center, June 27, 2016. "On Views of Race and Inequality, Blacks and Whites Are Worlds Apart."

42. C. M. Steele, and J. Aronson, J. (1995). Stereotype threat and the intellectual test performance of African Americans. *Journal of personality and social psychology, 69(5)*, 797.

43. Ibid.

44. T. R. Hurt (2014). Black men and the decision to marry. *Marriage & Family Review, 50*, 447–479. doi:10.1080/01494929.2014.905816.

Figure 27. Marriage

In the study, the men noted five factors that encouraged marriage: *wife's characteristics, spirituality, desire to be together, readiness to marry, and encouragement from others*. Five barriers to marriage were *personal reservations, perceived loss of freedom, disapproval from others, prior relationship experiences, and finances*. Forty-four percent reported they would marry at the same time if they had to make the choice to marry again, while 30% would opt to marry later, and 23% would select to marry earlier. Three percent of men would not choose to marry again.

According to Hurt (2014), the study's findings underscore the importance of love in the decision to marry, as 37% of the sample noted that they married because their wives complemented them well and embodied characteristics that were attractive to them (Coontz, 2005;[45] Lawson and Thompson,1999;[46]South, 1993[47]). Another

[45] S. Coontz (2005). Marriage, a history: From obedience to intimacy or how love conquered marriage. New York: Viking.

[46] E. J. Lawson, and A. Thompson (1999). Black men and divorce. Thousand Oaks, CA: Sage Publications.

[47] S. J. South (1993). For love or money? Sociodemographic determinants of the expected benefits of marriage. In S. J. South and S. E. Tolnay (eds.), The changing American family: Sociological and demographic perspectives. (pp. 171–194). Westview Press: Boulder, CO.

19% of the sample recalled the desire to be with their wives in their decision to marry. The men's comments reflect upon common themes in friendship-based love and romantic love, with friendship-based love as a "comfortable and affectionate" love for a partner (Grote and Frieze, 1994[48]), and romantic love comprising intimate and passionate components of love (Sternberg, 2004[49]).

Spirituality was also noted as a key factor for encouraging marriage among 27% of the men. Religiously-oriented persons are likely to view their marriages through a spiritual lens (Hopkins-Williams, 2007[50]). Moreover, religious affiliation has been found to promote marital formation (King & South, 2011[51]) (Figure 28).

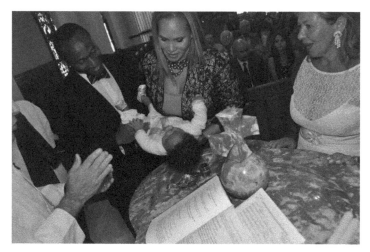

Figure 28. Spirituality.

48. N. K. Grote, and I. H. Frieze (1994). The measurement of friendship-based love in intimate relationships. Personal Relationships, 1, 275–300. doi: 10.1111/j.1475-6811.1994.tb00066.x.
49. R. J. Sternberg (2004). A triangular theory of love. In H. T. Reiss, and C. E. Rusbult (eds.), Close relationships: Key readings. (pp. 213–227). Philadelphia: Taylor & Francis.
50. K. Hopkins-Williams (2007). "Yes, they're out there": A qualitative study on strong African American marriages. (Unpublished doctoral dissertation). Louisiana State University and Agricultural and Mechanical College.
51. R. D. King, and S. J. South (2011). Crime, race, and the transition to marriage. Journal of Family Issues, 32 (1), 99–126. doi: 10.1177/0192513X10375059.

The men's perspectives that their marriages were a blessing to their lives were shaped by their religious beliefs and spirituality (Hurt, 2013[52]). The viewpoint that marriage was a gift from God probably aided in setting a firm base for the men's dedication to their wives (Lambert and Dollahite, 2008[53]). Another 19% of men spoke of their readiness to marry as the primary factor encouraging marriage to their wives.

Their reflections centered on the importance of individual development, maturity, and favorable perceptions about the benefits of marriage in the decision to marry. Previous work by Schneider (2011)[54] has noted the importance of men achieving specific milestones, e.g., working a steady job, securing financial assets prior to deciding to marry. Individual development proved to be a key obstacle for the men as they reflected upon the decision to marry, e.g., 27% personal reservations, 23% perceived loss of freedom, 10% prior relationship experiences.

Lack of preparedness for marriage in these areas was noted as barriers among the men. The men recalled being ready for the kind of commitment that marriage requires and a desire to begin a family with a spouse after having an opportunity to experience life and overcome their reservations about marriage, e.g., perceived loss of freedom, reduced availability of sex partners, limited opportunities to socialize with peers (Anderson, 1999[55]). Encouragement and support from family, close friends, and mentors was also regarded as a key factor in the decision to marry for 12% of men.

Strong ties to kin have been underscored in previous work as a key factor to consider in marital formation. Close relationships with

---

[52.] T. R. Hurt. (2014). Black men and the decision to marry. *Marriage & Family Review, 50,* 447–479. doi:10.1080/01494929.2014.905816.

[53.] N. M. Lambert, and D.C. Dollahite (2008). The threefold cord: Marital commitment in religious couples. Journal of Family Issues, 29, 592–614. doi:10.1177/0192513x07308395.

[54.] D. Schneider (2011). Wealth and the marital divide. American Journal of Sociology, 117 (2), 627–667.

[55.] E. Anderson (1999). Code of the street: Decency, violence, and the moral life of the inner city. New York: W. W. Norton.

extended family and allegiance to the family unit can promote the likelihood of marriage (Sassler and Goldscheider, 2004[56]). Extended family networks are very significant sources of social support for individuals, especially among blacks (Chatters, Taylor, and Jayakody, 1994[57]).

Conversely, these close ties could also dissuade someone from marrying or serve as a barrier to marriage, as was stated among 13% of the men. These findings corroborate previous empirical and theoretical work which points to the influential role of social networks on the course of a couple's relationship (Sprecher, 2010[58]). A small proportion of men (8%) cited finances as a barrier to marriage.

It was a barrier to marriage but was not cited among most men as a significant obstacle in the decision to marry. This could be attributable to the fact that the study employs a middle-class sample rather than a group of low-income men. Among the men, finances are described as a component of an overall readiness to marry.

*The previous study provides detailed rigor and results toward understanding the decision to marry among various black men. Based on the study and current **racial issues** in our country, I believe there are two **simplex factors** that are involved in a durable family unit: **1. INCOME** and **2. LOVE** (figure 29). Let's discuss **INCOME** first.*

56. S. Sassler, and F. Goldscheider (2004). Revisiting Jane Austen's theory of marriage timing changes in union formation among American men in the late 20th century. Journal of Family Issues, 25(2), 139–166.

57. L. M. Chatters, R. J. Taylor, and R. Jayakody, R. (1994). Fictive kinship relations in black extended families. Journal of Comparative Family Studies, 25(3), 297–312.

58. S. Sprecher (2010). The influence of social networks on romantic relationships: Through the lens of the social network. Personal Relationships, 18, 630–644. doi: 10.1111/j.1475-6811.2010.01330.x.

Figure 29. Love.

Income

INCOME is a vital aspect for forming a resilient foundation for a family. *When poverty rates are marginal within the family structure, parents can provide stable environments that foster positive emotional growth and well-being for their children.* I think everyone agrees with this logic, however, we have various ***disparities and differences*** on how income is achieved and who should bring the income.

*I believe that family **income** is an endured and shared responsibility between the family couple. Each member of the couple must prepare themselves **educationally and spiritually** toward achieving the necessary **expenditures** for obtaining and supporting a stable family structure.*

*For me, I had to complete my doctorate degree and improve my salary **before** I was **comfortable** toward starting a family and contributing to a family structure. **Why?** Because I knew I wasn't prepared financially and mentally (due to education fatigue) to contribute "**my share**" to a family structure until my degree was complete and my salary expectations were met.*

***Now, you are probably thinking "weak excuse," right? If two people love each other** (we haven't talked about love yet) **and are dedicated to starting a family, then the financial aspects of this decision will transpire naturally between the couple** (where there is a will, there is a way, right?).*

*I can certainly understand why people would think that. But building a family is like building a house. You must first create a **blueprint** (figure 30) on how to build a house. Once complete, then you need to validate the **blueprint** to make sure it is accurate.*

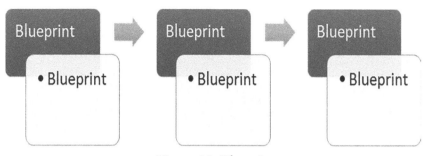

Figure 30. Blueprint

*Once the **blueprint** has been validated for accuracy, then you can begin building the house, based on the validated instructions of the **blueprint**. **No one builds a house without a blueprint, correct? Would you live in a house built without a blueprint?** Your answers to both questions are probably **no**.*

*So why build a "family" without a "**blueprint**"? You wouldn't, right? It is a straightforward question with a straightforward answer. But unfortunately, we constantly proceed in **trying to build families** without **validated** blueprints. Thus, we have no plans or instructions on how to properly construct our families.*

*To correct this problem, we need a "**family blueprint**" for our family structure. AND HERE IS THE GREAT NEWS! If you haven't started a **blueprint** already, you can start constructing your **blueprint** right now. Let's begin!*

Family Blueprint

*The first step in our "**family blueprint**" is to prepare a **strategy toward educating** ourselves (chapter 1) on obtaining **INCOME** to support a stable family structure. As mentioned in chapter 1, we must* *first adopt **humility** toward educating ourselves on "new" topics such as obtaining **INCOME**. We must then list **INCOME** as the topic of choice (figure 31).*

Figure 31. List the "Income" topic.

*We must then **ask ourselves, "Why do I need additional knowledge on obtaining INCOME?"** The purpose of this question is to really understand your **intentions** for learning this topic/subject (figure 32). In other words, **"How important is learning about obtaining INCOME to you?"***

*The answer should be simple. Obtaining **INCOME** is a vital aspect for forming a resilient foundation for a family. **Learning how** to obtain **INCOME** will **directly improve** yourself, your family, and your community (figure 32). Thus, learning about this topic would not be a **waste of your time**, and you should **invest a large amount of your time** in learning about this topic.*

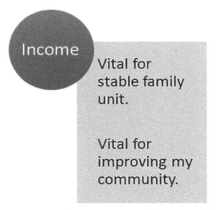

Figure 32. Importance of "income."

*The next step is **"Getting additional knowledge about obtaining INCOME."** We will use technologies like search engines for gather-*

ing additional information. Use your smartphone or go to your local library to access a computer with a "browser." Go to your favorite search engine.

*In the search box, type in the concise statement phrase **"obtaining good income."** The reason for **"a short statement phrase"** is so you don't end up with too many search results or too few results. Click the "Search" button.*

*Now, there will be several results that may peek your interest such as **"passive income ideas", "residual income ideas", and "college programs that render high salaries."** Certain college programs like Computer Science and Data Science for example, render high salaries applicable to supporting a stable family structure.*

*The last step, **"Execute training,"** involves implementing training toward obtaining **INCOME**. If college programs like computer science and data science are of interest, you will need to execute training to become skilled at these topics. This will involve searching and collecting information on colleges and funding options for paying college tuition. Your training will also be **ongoing** and will come from a variety of sources such as college courses, books, technical groups, the military, social groups, community programs, and conferences.*

*So figure 33 is what our **"family blueprint"** looks like so far with **INCOME**. Let's now talk about **LOVE** (figure 34) and how it plays into the blueprint. **LOVE** is a combination of different feelings related to profound affection.*

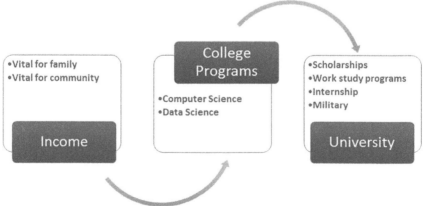

Figure 33. Family blueprint (income only).

Figure 34. Love.

It is also vital toward the resilient foundation of the family. I think everyone agrees that **LOVE** is a valued asset and may be the most important quality of a family. We as human beings, however, have various *inconsistencies and differences* on how to **LOVE**. *So what is the right way to LOVE?*

This is a **question for the ages**, and there is no right or wrong answers to this question. **Why?** Because we humans are different from one another, and we have distinct personal preferences and desires that influence our perspective and decisions on **LOVE**. *YEAH, YEAH, YEAH, WE KNOW THAT! (Smile.)*

SO BACK TO THE QUESTION (Smile). What is the right way to LOVE? Here are my thoughts.

We must try to **LOVE** each other with the same rigor and thoroughness as we **LOVE** ourselves (figure 35). **I KNOW, I KNOW,** that is tough because **not** everyone will **share** the same mind-set about **LOVE**. And no one wants to be a victim or casualty of a broken heart.

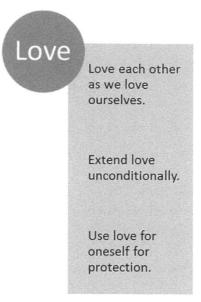

Figure 35. Importance of "Love" topic.

LOVING someone, however, requires you to extend your **LOVE** to others unconditionally, while using **LOVE** for oneself for protection. I have had several experiences in life in which I felt **LOVE** for another individual, however, overtime, their philosophy and perspective on giving and receiving **LOVE** changed. This was a difficult situation for me **(or for anyone)** to deal with, given that I was fully committed to the relationship and the person.

It takes time and patience to move on from a broken relationship, and the **LOVE** for myself allowed this to occur. It also allowed me to seek other avenues for **LOVE** and to discover new aspects about my character and my faith. So loving others with the same rigor and thoroughness as we **LOVE** ourselves allows us to grow into better people. When we evolve into better people, we become better family members, community leaders, and Americans.

Consequently, **LOVE** must be integrated into our *"family blueprint"* (figure 36). As shown in figure 36, **LOVE (pink)** is extended into each attribute of the blueprint, fueling the desire to obtain **INCOME** by means of college courses on the university level. Let's recap this section before moving into chapter 3, **Spirituality**.

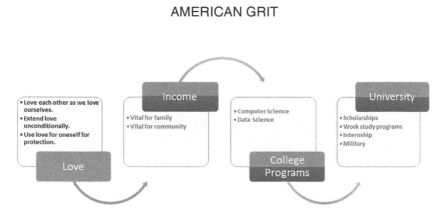

Figure 36. Family blueprint (love and income).

1. *There are two simplex factors that are involved in a durable family unit: INCOME and LOVE.*
2. A family blueprint is required toward depicting how *INCOME* and *LOVE* will be integrated for building the family structure.
3. The blueprint should constantly be analyzed and updated to reflect enduring changes to the family structure.

Got it? Good. Let's talk about *spirituality*.

Chapter 3

Spirituality

As mentioned earlier, African Americans are more religious on a variety of measures than the US population according to the US Religious Landscape Survey, conducted in 2007 by the Pew Research Center's Forum on Religion and Public Life (figure 37). Compared with other racial and ethnic groups, African Americans are among the most likely to report a formal religious affiliation. Eighty-seven percent of African Americans describe themselves as belonging to a religious group.

Figure 37. African-Americans and religion.

These metrics should not be surprising to anyone, given the **prolonged relationship** *between black people and the church toward confronting* **racism, disenfranchisement, poverty, and unemploy-**

*ment. **GRAB YOUR COFFEE!** The following article by the **African American Registry** titled "The Black Church: A Brief History"[59] provides comprehensive details about the relationship.*

During the decades of slavery in America, slave associations were a constant source of concern to slave owners. For many members of white society, Black religious meetings symbolized the ultimate threat to white existence. Nevertheless, African slaves established and relied heavily on their churches.[60] Religion offered a means of catharsis . . . Africans retained their faith in God and found refuge in their churches. However, white society was not always willing to accept the involvement of slaves in Christianity. As one slave recounted "the white folks would come in when the colored people would have prayer meeting, and whip every one of them. Most of them thought that when colored people were praying it was against them."

Religious exercises of slaves were closely watched to detect plans for escape or insurrection. African-American churches showed an air of militancy in the eyes of white Americans. Insurrections such as Nat Turner's in Virginia, born out of the religious inspiration of slaves, horrified white Americans. Understanding the potential end which could result from the religious experiences of African slaves, many white Americans opposed the participation of Blacks in Christianity. In African-American history, "the church" has long been at the center of Black communities. It has established itself as the greatest source for African American religious enrichment and secular development.

This development is embodied in Christianity, and the term, "the Black Church" presents many details of racial

---

59. African American Registry. (2017). "The Black Church," A Brief History. Available at http://www.aaregistry.org/historic_events/view/black-church-brief-history.

60. The Center for African American Ministries and Black Church Studies, 5460 South University Avenue, Chicago, IL 60615, V: 773-947-6300.

and religious lifestyles unique to Black history. The term "the Black Church" is a misnomer. It implies that all Black churches share or have shared the same aspirations and strategies for creating cohesive African-American communities. This is not true, and there were numerous differences found among Black communities which were reflected within their community churches. Black communities differed from region to region. They were divided along social lines, composed of persons from different economic levels, and maintained varying political philosophies. Black communities in the inner cities of the United States have traditionally differed from those in rural areas, etc. In the Negro Church in America, the sociologist E. Franklin Frazier noted, "Methodist and Baptist denominations were separate church organizations based upon distinctions of color and what were considered standards of civilized behavior."

Organized politically and spiritually, black churches were not only given to the teachings of Christianity but they were faithfully relied upon to address the specific issues which affected their members.[61] For many African-American Christians, regardless of their denominational differences, Black Churches have always represented their religion, community, and home. Scholars have repeatedly asserted that Black history and Black church history overlap enough to be virtually identical. One of the First known Black churches in America was created before the American Revolution, around 1758. Called the African Baptist or "Bluestone" Church, this house of worship was founded on the William Byrd plantation near the Bluestone River, in Mecklenburg, Virginia. Africans at the time believed that only adult baptism by total immersion was doctrinally correct.

Black people in America also supported the autonomy of their congregation to make decisions independent of

---

[61.] Marvin Andrew McMickle (2002). *An Encyclopedia of African American Christian Heritage*. Judson Press.

larger church body. Other early Black Church milestones included the Baptist and Episcopal denominations. The First African Baptist Church of Savannah, Georgia, which began in 1777. This is said to be the oldest Black church in North America. Originally called the First Colored Church the pastoral life of George Leile's preaching is tied to its beginning.

In 1787, Blacks in Philadelphia organized the Free African Society, the first organized Afro-American society, and Absalom Jones and Richard Allen were elected as overseers. They established contact and created relationships with similar Black groups in other cities. Five years later, the Society began to build a church, which was dedicated on July 17, 1794. The African Church applied for membership in the Episcopal Diocese of Pennsylvania. The end of the Confederacy signaled freedom for millions of southern black slaves and prompted the emancipation of the black church. This started the emergence of the black church as a separate institution.

At the time, white southerners still sought to maintain control over African Americans' worship, for both religious and social reasons. Such services typically emphasized the responsibility of the slave to be obedient and provided biblical justification for black bondage. Slaves had no voice in church affairs and were relegated to the rear of the church or the gallery, as spectators rather than full members of the congregation.

Post-Civil War: After emancipation, black churches became virtually the only place for African Americans to find refuge. Blacks moved away from the "hush-harbors" that they retreated to for solace as slaves. Formally during this time, a church separation petition was filed by thirty-eight black members of the predominantly white Fairfield Baptist Church in Northumberland County, Virginia, in 1867. Referring to the new political and social status of African Americans, the petitioners said they wanted to "place ourselves where we could best promote our mutual good" and suggested "a separate church organization as the best possible way. A month later the white members of the church unanimously acceded to the petitioners' request, setting the stage for the creation of the all-black Shiloh Baptist Church."

Once established, Black Churches spread rapidly throughout the South; the Baptist churches led in this proliferation. The 1800s ushered in many millstones that built on the foundation of the Black Church. To mention just a few, 1808 celebrated the founding of Abyssinian Baptist Church in New York City. Black Americans along with a group of Ethiopian merchants were unwilling to accept racially segregated seating of the First Baptist Church of New York City. They withdrew forever their membership and established themselves in a building on Anthony Street (later Worth Street) calling it the Abyssinian Baptist Church. The name was inspired by the nation from which the merchants of Ethiopia had come, Abyssinia.

Other new churches also emerged because of the missionary activities of black ministers. The Reverend Alexander Bettis, a former South Carolina slave, alone organized more than forty Baptist churches between 1865 and his death in 1895.

Services: With the division of congregations came the development of a distinct religious observance combining elements of African ritual, slave emotionalism, southern suffering, and individual eloquence. Working-class Baptist and Methodist church services fused African and European forms of religious expression to produce a unique version of worship that reflected the anguish, pain, and occasional elation of nineteenth-century black life in the United States.

Such services usually involved a devotional prayer provided by a leading member of the church, singing by the congregation and choir, and the minister's sermon. The prayer would request a powerful God to ease the earthly burden of the congregation and would be enhanced by the congregation's response, an expression of agreement with the words "Yes, Lord," "Have mercy, Lord," and "Amen."

After the prayer, the congregation typically showed their devotion through song. Even if a formal choir existed, all the members of the congregation would be expected to participate. Occasionally an individual member outside the choir would stand up and lead the house in song. By the turn of the century, most southern black church choirs had assumed the responsibility for presenting the hymns, but the "call and response" tradition continues today.

The third element in a classic black service was the minister's sermon. Building on the long tradition of slave preachers and "exhorters," many ministers employed all the drama and poetry at their command, injecting vivid imagery and analogy into their biblical accounts conveying understanding of the rewards of righteousness and the wages of sin. Not every minister can elicit such a response. But those ministers who did avoid "emotion without substance" and stirred their congregations to strive for a more profound faith and more righteous way of living in a world of adversity provided spiritual guidance for a people whose faith and capacity for forgiveness was tested daily. For these people the black church was indeed "a rock in a weary land."

Nineteenth-century black churches ministered to the needs of the soul and served a host of secular functions, which placed them squarely in the center of black social life. Church buildings doubled as community meeting centers and schools until permanent structures could be built, and during Reconstruction they served as political halls. The black church provided shelter for visitors as well as temporary community theaters and concert halls where religious and secular plays and programs were presented.

In a blurring of spiritual and social functions church members provided care for the sick or incapacitated and financial assistance to students bound for college. They also sponsored virtually all the many fraternal lodges that emerged in the nineteenth-century South. As racially motivated violence and terrorism ran rampant across the country, Black churches were staunch in their resistance.

In 1886 blacks organized the National Baptist Convention, in a continued attempt to reduce the influence of white national bodies among blacks. As the number of Baptist churches grew, they met regularly in regional conventions that then evolved into statewide and national organizations. By 1895 the various Baptist associations had formed the National Baptist Convention of America, representing 3 million African American Baptists, primarily in the South.

The African Methodist Episcopal (AME) Church emerged as the second-largest, post-Civil War black denomination. Because of its independence, the AME Church had always been viewed with suspicion in the antebellum South, having been forced out of South Carolina following the Denmark Vesey conspiracy of 1822. The church was reorganized in South Carolina in 1865 by Bishop Daniel Payne and grew to forty-four thousand members by 1877. Similar growth in other southern states gave the AME Church by 1880 a national membership of four hundred thousand its followers were for the first time concentrated in the South.

Other denominations completed the spectrum of black church organization in the South. The Colored Methodist Episcopal (now Christian Methodist Episcopal) Church, which grew from the black parishioners who withdrew in 1866 from the predominantly white Methodist Episcopal Church, and the African Methodist Episcopal Zion Church each claimed two hundred thousand members by 1880.

In 1895, a meeting attended by more than 2000 clergy was held in Atlanta, Georgia. The three largest conventions of the day: the Baptist Foreign Missionary Convention, the American National Baptist Convention and the

National Baptist Educational Convention merged to form the National Baptist Convention of the United States of America. This brought both northern and southern black Baptist churches together. Among the delegates was Rev. A. D. Williams, pastor of the Ebenezer Baptist Church and grandfather of the Rev. Martin Luther King, Jr.

However, the more involved Black Churches became in sparring against the racial intolerance and violence targeted against them, the more the churches and their members were punished. Within the church the Presbyterians and Episcopalians also saw the division of their memberships into white and black denominations, with each of the two black churches having some one hundred thousand members by 1900.

In 1908, The Christian Index published the "Colored Methodist Bishops' Appeal to White America – 1908." In their statement, church leaders responded to the surge of mob violence and lynching occurring across the country, denouncing terrorism waged against Black persons and imploring the country to suppress the spread of anti-Black violence. As anti-Black terrorism proliferated into the twentieth century, Black churches grew increasingly vehement in their calls for castigation of racial violence. Also on September 15, 1915, the National Baptist Convention of America was formed.

Between World War I and World War II, the black church continued to be not only an arena of social and political life for the leaders of blacks; it had a political meaning for the masses. Although they were denied the right to vote in the American community, within their churches, especially the Methodist Churches, they could vote and engage in electing their officers. The election of bishops and other officers and representatives to conventions has been a serious activity for the masses of blacks.

Almost a century ago the Black church was an organizational site for social and political activities, centers for economic development and growth. As microcosms of the larger society, Black churches provided an environment free of oppression and racism for African Americans. In black churches, African Americans were consistently exposed to social, political, and economic opportunities which could be sought and had by all members equally. The representational structure of African-American churches confirmed Black preachers as both religious and community leaders. The sermons of many Black preachers expounded messages of Christianity analogized to the daily experiences of African Americans. Thematic expressions of overcoming oppression and "lifting while climbing," were first articulated in church sermons.

Civil Right Era: During the Civil Rights era, Black churches were well established social and political power bases for African Americans. Their enormous presence naturally, sanctioned them with the political power to lead Black people in the movement for civil rights. Some churches and their organizations were completely opposed to any involvement in the political struggle for civil rights. Others chose to participate and did so passionately, organizing by rallies, protests, and marches, while teaching Christianity and community involvement.

In the late 1940s, '50s, and '60s, the Black Church functioned as the institutional center for Black mobilization. They provided an organizational base and meeting place, for African Americans to strategize their moves in the ongoing fight against racial segregation and oppression. As Black Churches became the epicenter of the social and political struggles for Black equality, they increasingly became targets for racially motivated violence. An extensive assault on members of a Black community took place by burning a Black Church.

The bombing and burning of Black churches during this time translated into an attack upon the core of civil rights activism, as well as upon the larger Black religious community. The most infamous example of racist American church destruction occurred on September 15, 1963. When the Sixteenth Street Baptist Church in Birmingham, Alabama, was fire bombed, the explosion was felt by the entire Black community. Four children killed in the attack, several others injured, and a community's sense of security within their church was forever traumatized.

This act signified the depths to which racial hatred could fall. Like many other churches bombed before and after, the Sixteenth Street Baptist Church was a Black Church. Even though the KKK was implicated in this crime, members of the KKK were not the only ones responsible for similar acts of terror throughout the country. Unfortunately, this was not an isolated incident. These, racially motivated arsons did not destroy the souls of Black communities. In 1988, the National Missionary Baptist Convention of America was formed.

In the 1990 C. Eric Lincoln book The Black Church in the African American Experience with Lawrence H. Mamiya. They described the, "seven major historic black denominations: the African Methodist Episcopal (AME) Church; the African Methodist Episcopal Zion (AMEZ) Church; the Christian Methodist Episcopal (CME) Church; the National Baptist Convention, USA., Incorporated (NBC); the National Baptist Convention of America, Unincorporated (NBCA); the Progressive National Baptist Convention (PNBC); and the Church of God in Christ (COGIC)," as comprising "The Black Church."

In the Twenty-first century, the Convention movement of the African American Baptist Church has undergone several changes, the individual organizations remain important to African American religious life. The Black Church is also at a crossroads dude to "White Flight," gentrification and systemic capitalism. The Black Church has historically been a source of hope and strength for the African American community.

*The previous article provides a **GREAT** narrative on the **prolonged relationship** between black people and the church toward confronting **racism, disenfranchisement, poverty, and unemployment.** Furthermore, the article explains how churches provided communal worship, centers for political organization, and black ministers for community leadership. With this detailed background in mind, let's explore the **SPIRITUAL** aspect of the **AMERICAN GRIT** model.*

Spiritual Aspect of American Grit

*I believe that **SPIRITUALITY** (figure 38) involves connecting to a belief that is **BIGGER** than ourselves and **GREATER** than diseases and sicknesses like **RACISM, INEQUALITY, and DISCRIMINATION**. For most Americans, this involves associating with a religious principle such as Christianity, Muslim, Judaism, etc. Religion, like other convictions, requires patrons to have **FAITH** in the principles and ideas that make up the creed.*

Figure 38. Spirituality

FAITH is the belief in a religion based on **no or diminutive** *proof, but instead, on divine conviction. My father, the minister, would say "having* ***FAITH*** *is good, but* ***FAITH*** *without consciousness about your own imperfections is* ***DANGEROUS.*** *" It took me a while to fully understand what my father meant by this statement, but I get it now* **(Thanks, Dad).**

Let me explain. *As we search for spiritual answers within our religions, we must keep in mind that our imperfections influence our* ***FAITH*** *on what we* ***THINK*** *is right and wrong. So if we are lacking in* ***EDUCATION, LOVE,*** *or strong* ***FAMILY*** *ties, these deficiencies skew our* ***FAITH*** *on what is moral and what is not. Many Americans who practice* **racism and discrimination** *truly have* ***FAITH*** *in what they believe, however, their* ***FAITH is*** *warped by their imperfections.*

Their imperfections are applied to their ***FAITH*** *intuitively, thus, creating aspiration, ambition, and morally toward practicing* **racism and discrimination**. *This concept is not just limited to Americans who are racist, this notion is* **universal** *and is* **applicable** *to different scenarios based on the imperfections of the individuals.* **So how do we prevent this from happening?**

Simple answer. You ready? Whenever you ***BEGIN*** *to place your* ***FAITH*** *into a conviction, principle, or idea, ask yourself the following questions:*

1. Does the conviction, principle, or idea involve *LOVE* for myself, my family, my friends, and my colleagues of different races? *It's no coincidence that* **love** *is common in all religions.* **Most religions teach that the greatest mandate is to love one another.**

2. Does the conviction, principle, or idea involve *JOY for* myself, my family, my friends, and my colleagues of different races? *Most religions teach about enduring joy during good and bad times.*

3. Does the conviction, principle, or idea involve *PEACE* for myself, my family, my friends, and my colleagues of different races? *Again, most religions focus on peace through prayer and networking with other divine groups.*

4. Does the conviction, principle, or idea involve **ENLIGHTENING** myself, my family, and my colleagues of different races? *Most religions teach about educating each other on various topics toward improving ourselves, e.g., financial matters, parenthood, etc.*

The analysis for evaluating your chosen conviction, principle, or idea is certainly **NOT** limited to my recommended questions above however, my questions are a **STARTING POINT** for you to conduct a **DETAILED** evaluation of your religion. **KEEP IN MIND,** my questions are based on the premise of my father, the minister, in which our belief is, **"Religion is supposed to bring human beings together, not separate."**

Upon completing your analysis, you **MUST** apply your chosen religion or belief to your **"blueprint." REMEMBER the BLUEPRINT!** So figure 39 is what our revised, final **"blueprint"** looks like with the addition of **RELIGION.**

Consequently, **LOVE and RELIGION** *is fully integrated into our "family blueprint" (figure 39).* As shown in figure 39, **LOVE (pink) and RELIGION (green)** is extended into each attribute of the blueprint, fueling the desire to obtain **INCOME** by means of college courses on the university level. Let's recap this section before moving into the final chapter.

1. **SPIRITUALITY** *involves connecting to a belief that is* **BIGGER** *than ourselves and* **GREATER** *than diseases and sicknesses like* **RACISM, INEQUALITY, and DISCRIMINATION.**

2. *Having* **FAITH** *is good, but* **FAITH** *without consciousness about your own imperfections is* **"DANGEROUS."**

3. *Whenever you* **BEGIN** *to place your* **FAITH** *into a conviction, principle, or idea, ask yourself my* **RECOMMENDED** *questions listed in this chapter.*

4. *Religion is supposed to bring human beings together, not separate.*

Okay. On to chapter 4, "Who's Got American GRIT?"

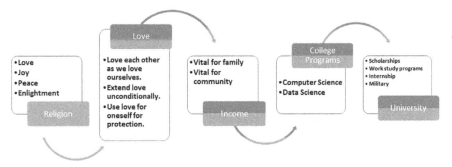

Figure 39. Final family blueprint (religion and love).

Finale

Who's Got American Grit?

As we near the conclusion of this book, I would like to provide you some last thoughts. We must continue to **HEAL** *and* **PROGRESS** *from our* **SICKNESS** *of* **RACISM and INEQUALITY** *in America so that we become a* **COUNTRY OF ONE.** *Not a country of blacks, not a country of whites, not a country of Latinos, etc., but a* **COUNTRY OF ONE.**

AMERICAN GRIT (figure 40) is a cure for the sickness of **RACISM** *and* **INEQUALITY.** *It is also a method for confronting* **RACISM and INEQUALITY** *and a technique for building a* **COUNTRY OF ONE.** *By surrounding yourself with* **education, spirituality, and family,** **contentment** *is achieved for yourself, your family, and your colleagues.*

This is critical to **ALL AMERICANS, but vital** *to* **high-risk** communities *who are greatly impacted by* **racism, disenfranchisement, poverty, and unemployment.**

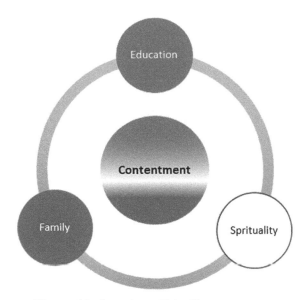

Figure 40. American Grit: Contentment =
education + spirituality + family.

Everyday people like you and myself are the ones that can imple-ment AMERICAN GRIT into our way of life. "MAKING AMERICA GREAT AGAIN" doesn't happen by merely electing a specific person to the White House and hoping this person can perform a miracle. We, the *everyday people of America,* are responsible for leading and influenc-ing the **GREATNESS** of America.

We are responsible for safeguarding our country from internal and external terrorism and cyber attacks that damage our way of life. To achieve these goals, we must collectively work **TOGETHER** as one. *Everyday people* with *everyday actions* that influence America with *AMERICA GRIT.*

Thank you for listening to my **BATTLE CRY.** I leave you with a few inspiring **everyday AMERICANS** who possess **AMERICAN GRIT.** Their **everyday actions** have advanced our American way of life, and their stories should be told, not overshadowed. Let's start with *Sylvia Mendez.*

Sylvia Mendez[62]

Sylvia Mendez is the daughter of Gonzalo Mendez, a Mexican immigrant, and Felicitas Mendez, a Puerto Rican immigrant, who fought so that Sylvia could have an equal education through the landmark court case battle of Mendez v. Westminster, et al. In 1943, students of Mexican decent were required to enroll in separate schools from Caucasian children. When Sylvia was in third grade, she and her siblings were denied admission to the segregated, "white school" near their Orange County home.

The Mendez family fought back. Their 1947 victory desegregated public schools in California and became an example for broader decisions, such as the Brown v. Board of education. Sylvia Mendez's sole intent is to convey the importance of obtaining an education by encouraging students to stay in school and continue their education.

Case Details

In September 1943, Sylvia Mendez, then nine years old, and her two brothers went with their aunt and three cousins to enroll at the 17th Street School in Westminster. School officials, however, told her aunt that her children, who were half-Mexican but had light skin and a French surname, could register at the "white" elementary school. The Mendez kids, who were dark-skinned and had a Mexican last name, were not allowed; they had to enroll at the "Mexican" school ten blocks away.

Mendez's parents were appalled and sued the school district in what turned out to be a groundbreaking civil rights case that helped outlaw almost a hundred years of segregation in California and was a precedent seven years later for Brown v. Board of Education.

"I didn't realize registering for school would have such an impact," says Mendez, seventy-one, who now lives in Fullerton.

[62.] Sylvia Mendez (2017). Sylvia Mendez. Available at http://sylviamendezinthe-mendezvswestminster.com.

Segregation was standard practice in 1940s California (Asian and Native American children also attended separate schools), but it wasn't always the case. When California Constitution was drafted in 1849, Spanish and English were the state's official languages.

Previous to 1855, Mexican children attended Anglo schools. But after the Mexican-American War and the Treaty of Guadalupe Hidalgo, which ceded California, Arizona, New Mexico, and Colorado to the United States, was signed, the state legislature changed a few laws. In 1855, the state legislature said school boards could not use public funds to educate non-white students. In 1864, non-white students were educated in segregated schools.

Until the Mendez case, the logic of "separate but equal" facilities, which was established by the US Supreme Court in the 1896 case of Plessy v. Ferguson, was the law of the land. The Mendez family (father Gonzalo, mother Felicitas, sons Gonzalo Jr. and Jerome, and daughter Sylvia) moved from Santa Ana, where they owned a cafe, to Westminster, where they leased a ranch from the Munemitsus, a Japanese family who was being interned at Poston, Arizona. When Gonzalo was told his children were barred from the 17th Street School, he talked with the superintendent and then went to the Orange County School District. They rejected his requests that his children be allowed to enroll.

The Mendez family, who had become successful tenant farmers in Westminster, hired David Marcus, a Los Angeles civil rights attorney, to sue the Westminster school district. But Marcus made a bigger case, and on March 2, 1945, filed Mendez v. Westminster, a class-action lawsuit against four Orange County school districts (Westminster, Santa Ana, Garden Grove, and El Modena, now Eastern Orange) seeking an injunction that would order the schools to integrate. Friends of the court briefs in favor of desegregation were filed by the American Civil Liberties Union, National Association for the Advancement of Colored People, the National Lawyers Guild, the American Jewish Congress, and the Japanese American Citizens League.

The plaintiffs were five Mexican-American families (Mendez, Thomas Estrada, William Guzman, Frank Palomino, and Lorenzo Ramirez) on behalf of five thousand similarly situated children. Sylvia said she wasn't surprised by her father's actions.

"It was during the war when people were accused of being a communist if you didn't follow what was right, but he wasn't scared," she says. "He knew that what he was doing was the right thing to do. He was going to right a wrong." The trial started on July 5 in the US Federal District Court in Los Angeles. Marcus argued that the Mexican children were not treated equally by attending inferior schools with substandard books.

Marcus also argued that the Mexican children were not given adequate language testing before inclusion in the "Mexican" schools, and that segregation based on nationality violated the equal protection clause under the Fourteenth Amendment of the US Constitution. The school districts' lawyer, on the other hand, said education was a state matter and the federal courts had no jurisdiction. He also argued that students were segregated so Mexican students could receive English lessons that would ready them for immersion with the already fluent English students.

On March 18, 1946, Judge Paul J. McCormick ruled that the "segregation prevalent in the defendant school districts foster antagonisms in the children and suggest inferiority among them where none exists" and that the equal protection clause had been violated. "That was radical for the time," says Chris Arriola, a Santa Clara County deputy district attorney, who has written extensively on the Mendez v. Westminster case. "That decision overturned a law that said segregation was okay."

The school districts appealed the decision, but on April 14, 1947, the Ninth Circuit Court of Appeals in San Francisco upheld the federal court ruling. Shortly thereafter, California Gov. Earl Warren pushed the state legislature into repealing laws that segregated Asians and Native American school children. Mendez v. Westminster also paved the way for another historic civil rights trial.

Robert Smalls[63]

Robert Smalls (figure 41) was an enslaved African American who became a politician, serving in both the South Carolina legislature and the US House of Representatives. As a slave, Robert escaped to freedom in a Confederate supply ship and eventually became a sea captain for the Union Navy. After the war, he became a successful businessman and politician serving in both houses of the South Carolina legislature.

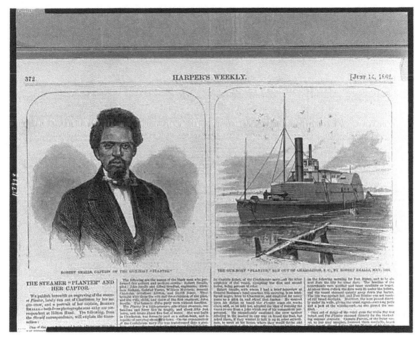

Figure 41. Robert Smalls, S.C. M.C. Born in Beaufort, SC, April 1839. (Library of Congress, prints and photographs division).

He was elected to the US House of Representatives in 1875 but was convicted of taking a bribe while in the state senate and sentenced to prison before he was pardoned by the governor. Robert

---

63. Robert Smalls (2017). Biography. Available at https://www.biography.com/people/robert-smalls-9486288.

Smalls was born to a house slave, Lydia Polite, in Beaufort, South Carolina, on April 5, 1839. The identity of his father is not officially known, but believed to be Henry McKee, the son of the plantation's owner.

Smalls was raised in the McKee house and enjoyed a little more acceptance in the community. On several occasions, he ignored the night curfew for blacks and stayed out with his white companions, much to his mother's lament. When Smalls was twelve, the McKee family moved to Charleston, where Smalls was hired as a day laborer on the waterfront, working as a rigger and eventually a sailor. In 1856, he married Hannah Jones, a slave hotel maid who worked in Charleston. Jones already had one daughter, and together she and Smalls had a daughter and a son, Robert Jr., who later died of smallpox.

Small's attempts to buy his wife and family out of slavery failed. At the outbreak of the Civil War, in March 1861, Robert Smalls was hired as a deckhand on the Confederate supply ship the *Planter*, a converted cotton steamer that carried supplies between forts in Charleston Harbor. Over the course of several months, Smalls learned all he could about navigating the ship and waited for an opportunity to escape.

In the predawn hours of May 13, 1862, while the white officers and crew slept in Charleston, Smalls and a crew of eight men, along with five women and three children (including Small's wife and two children), quietly slipped the *Planter* out of Charleston Harbor. Over the next few hours, Smalls successfully navigated the ship through five checkpoints, offering the correct signal to pass each, and then headed out to open waters and the Union blockade. It was daring and dangerous, and if caught, the crew was prepared to blow up the vessel.

The startled crew of the USS *Onward*, the first ship in the blockade to spot the *Planter*, almost fired on it before Smalls had the Confederate flag struck and raised a white bedsheet, signaling surrender. The ship's treasure of guns, ammunition, and important documents proved to be a wealth of information, telling the Union commanders of shipping routes, mine locations, and the times that

Confederate ships docked and departed. The story of the courageous escape of Robert Smalls became a national phenomenon and was one of the factors encouraging President Abraham Lincoln to authorize free African Americans to serve in the Union military.

Congress bestowed a $1,500 cash prize on Smalls, and he went on a speaking tour, recounting his heroics and recruiting African Americans to serve in the Union army. During the rest of the war, Smalls balanced his role as a spokesperson and Union navy captain on the *Planter* and the ironclad USS *Keokuk,* conducting seventeen missions in and around Charleston. After the war, Robert Smalls was commissioned as a brigadier general in the South Carolina militia and purchased his former owner's house in Beaufort, South Carolina.

He generously took in some of the McKee family, who were destitute. Smalls started a general store, a school for African American children, and a newspaper. His success opened doors in politics, and soon he served as a delegate to the state's constitutional convention and was elected to both the South Carolina House of Representatives and the state senate.

Between 1874 and 1879, he served in the United States House of Representatives, but his tenure was marred by partisan accusations that he took a $5,000 bribe while in the state senate. In 1877 Smalls was convicted of the offense and sentenced to three years in prison. Smalls was released pending his appeal, however, and in 1879, he was pardoned by the governor.

After his first wife's death in 1883, Robert Smalls remarried in 1890. He served as a US Customs collector in Beaufort from 1889 to 1911 and remained active in politics. Smalls died of natural causes in his Beaufort home on February 23, 1915, at age seventy-five.

Morris Dees[64]

Civil rights lawyer Morris Dees cofounded the Southern Poverty Law Center (SPLC), which addresses cases of racial discrimination and combats the power of hate groups. Attorney Morris Dees was born on December 16, 1936, in Shorter, Alabama. In 1971, Dees cofounded the SPLC.

The SPLC gained attention for its innovative tactics against hate groups, such as filing civil suits, claiming damages for the violence incited by these groups. After the 1981 lynching of Michael Donald, the SPLC helped his mother receive a $7 million judgment.

Civil rights lawyer Morris Dees was born Morris Seligman Dees Jr. on December 16, 1936, in Shorter, Alabama.

He was the oldest of five children. Dees's parents were tenant farmers who also operated a cotton gin. Dees was a resourceful child. At a young age, he started earning money by buying, rearing, and selling pigs. As a teen, he sold scraps from his parents' cotton gin as mulch.

Dees managed to accumulate approximately $5,000 in savings by the time he graduated from high school in 1955. At his parents' urging, Dees enrolled at the University of Alabama, where he would earn both his undergraduate and law degrees. In 1956, while he was an undergraduate, Dees witnessed crowds of white people—including members of the Ku Klux Klan—verbally and physi-cally harass Autherine Lucy, a classmate who was the first African American to attend the University of Alabama.

The scene revolted Dees and would resonate with him in the years to come. While he was still in school, Dees teamed up with a friend, Millard Fuller, to start a direct-mail business. When Dees graduated from law school in 1960, he and Fuller formed their own law practice in Montgomery, Alabama.

[64.] Morris Dees (2017). Biography. Available at https://www.biography.com/people/morris-dees-21415735.

They also grew their business, Fuller and Dees Marketing, to include a multimillion-dollar publishing venture. Dees bought out Fuller's share of the business in 1965. Stuck at an airport one night, Dees happened to read Clarence Darrow's autobiography, a book that would change the direction of his career.

In his own autobiography, *A Season for Justice* (1991), Dees explained, "I had made up my mind. I would sell the company as soon as possible and specialize in civil rights law. All the things in my life that had brought me to this point, all the pulls and tugs of my conscience, found a singular peace."

After deciding to refocus his career, Dees handled cases such as filing a suit to integrate Montgomery's YMCA. In 1969, he sold his company for several million dollars, which gave him more time to defend others' civil rights. In 1971, Dees worked with fellow attorney Joseph J. Levin Jr. and civil rights activist Julian Bond to found the SPLC.

Based in Montgomery, the not-for-profit agency was formed to "combat hate, intolerance, and discrimination through education and litigation." While at the SPLC, Dees worked on a strategy of filing civil suits against hate groups, claiming damages for the violence incited by these groups. One high-profile case where he applied this strategy was the 1981 lynching of Michael Donald, a crime committed by three Klan members.

With the assistance of Dees and the SPLC, Donald's mother was awarded a $7 million settlement from the United Klans of America, bankrupting the group. Over the years, the kinds of cases Dees handled led to his receiving death threats, but that has not kept him from continuing to investigate hate activity throughout the United States. In a 2009 letter to Congress, Dees requested that measures be taken to prevent members of extremist groups from serving in the military. In 2012, Dees was awarded the American Bar Association's ABA Medal for his dedication to the pursuit of tolerance, justice, and equality.

Viola Gregg Liuzzo[65]

Viola Gregg Liuzzo (figure 42) was an activist in the civil rights movement in the 1960s. She was murdered by members of the Ku Klux Klan for her efforts. Viola Gregg Liuzzo traveled to Alabama in March 1965 to help the Southern Christian Leadership Conference, led by Rev. Martin Luther King Jr., with its efforts to register African American voters in Selma.

Figure 42. Memorial to Viola Gregg Liuzzo.

Not long after her arrival, Liuzzo was murdered by members of the Ku Klux Klan while driving a black man from Montgomery to Selma. She was the only known white female killed during the civil rights movement.

---

65. Viola Gregg Liuzzo (2017). Biography. Available at https://www.biography.com/people/viola-gregg-liuzzo-370152.

Civil rights worker Viola Gregg Liuzzo was born Viola Gregg on April 11, 1925, in California, Pennsylvania, part of Washington County.

Viola Gregg Liuzzo traveled to Alabama in March 1965 to help the Southern Christian Leadership Conference, led by Rev. Martin Luther King Jr., with its efforts to register African American voters in Selma. Not long after her arrival, she was murdered by members of the Ku Klux Klan. Before heading to Selma, Liuzzo had lived in Detroit with her second husband, an official with the Teamsters union, and her five children (two from a previous marriage).

Her decision to go to Alabama was driven in part by the events of March 7, 1965, in Selma, also known as "Bloody Sunday." On that day, approximately six hundred civil rights supporters attempted to march from Selma to Montgomery along Highway 80. The group barely got started when they were attacked by state and local police officers on the Edmund Pettus Bridge using clubs and tear gas.

Liuzzo had watched the brutal assault on the protesters in a news broadcast and felt compelled to find a way to join the fight for civil rights. Politically and socially active, Liuzzo was a member of the Detroit chapter of the National Association for the Advancement of Colored People. She knew firsthand about the racial injustices that African Americans often suffered in the South, having spent some of her youth in Tennessee and Georgia, among other places.

Liuzzo may have been aware of the some of the dangers associated with social activism. On March 9, 1965, Martin Luther King Jr. had again attempted to march to Montgomery from Selma with more than 1,500 other civil rights advocates. King decided to return to Selma, however, after encountering the state police along the way.

That night in Selma, a white minister named James Reeb was beaten to death by a group of segregationists. On March 21, 1965, more than three thousand marchers led by Martin Luther King Jr. began their trek from Selma to Montgomery to campaign for voting rights for African Americans in the South. Unlike previous attempts, activists on this march were protected from outside interference by US Army and National Guard troops.

In addition to participating in the march, Liuzzo helped by driving supporters between Selma and Montgomery. The group reached Montgomery on March 25, 1965, and King gave a speech on the steps of the state capitol building to a crowd of approximately twenty-five thousand people. That night, Liuzzo was driving another civil rights worker with the SCLC, an African-American teenager named Leroy Moton, back to Selma on Highway 80, when another car pulled alongside her vehicle.

One of the passengers in the neighboring car shot at Liuzzo, striking her in the face and killing her. The car ended up in a ditch, and Moton survived the attack by pretending to be dead. The following day, President Lyndon B. Johnson appeared on television to announce that Liuzzo's killers had been caught.

The police arrested four members of the Ku Klux Klan for the killing: Eugene Thomas, Collie Leroy Wilkins Jr., William O. Eaton, and Gary Thomas Rowe (who was later revealed to be an FBI informant). Michigan Governor George Romney visited with Liuzzo's family after the murder and stated that Liuzzo "gave her life for what she believed in, and what she believed in is the cause of humanity everywhere," according to an article in the *New York Times*.

On March 30, 1965, roughly 350 people attended Liuzzo's funeral in Detroit, including Martin Luther King Jr., United Automobile Workers Union President Walter P. Reuther, Jimmy Hoffa of the International Brotherhood of Teamsters, and United States Attorney Lawrence Gubow.

Not long after her death, however, came a campaign to tarnish her reputation, driven by J. Edgar Hoover, director of the FBI. Assorted false stories were leaked that she was involved with Moton and that she was a bad wife and mother. Eugene Thomas, Collie Leroy Wilkins Jr., and William O. Eaton were first represented by Matt H. Murphy, a lawyer for the Ku Klux Klan. After Murphy died in a car accident, former Birmingham mayor Art Hanes took over the case.

The defendants were acquitted by an all-white jury on state charges related to the crime, though they were later convicted on federal charges. Thomas and Wilkins were sentenced to ten years in prison. Eaton died before his sentencing.

Rowe had immunity from prosecution and went into the witness protection program. Thomas and Wilkins later named Rowe as the shooter and he was indicted on murder charges, but they were dismissed because of his immunity deal. Despite the efforts to discredit Liuzzo, her murder led President Lyndon B. Johnson to order an investigation into the Ku Klux Klan.

It is also believed that her death helped encourage legislators to pass the Voting Rights Act of 1965. Liuzzo's story has been the subject of several books, including Mary Stanton's *From Selma to Sorrow: The Life and Death of Viola Liuzzo* (1998). In 2004, Paola di Florio showed her documentary on Liuzzo, *Home of the Brave*, at the Sundance Film Festival.

The critically acclaimed film explored Liuzzo's story as well as the impact of her murder on her children. The children had sued the federal government over her murder, but their case was eventually dismissed. Years after her vicious murder, Liuzzo received some recognition for her personal sacrifice.

She is among the forty civil rights martyrs honored on the Civil Rights Memorial in Montgomery, which was created in 1989. Two years later, the Women of the Southern Christian Leadership Conference placed a marker where she was killed on Highway 80. Liuzzo was also inducted into the Michigan Hall of Fame in 2006.

Faith Ringgold[66]

Faith Ringgold (figure 43) is an American artist and author who became famous for innovative, quilted narrations like *Tar Beach* that communicate her political beliefs. Faith Ringgold was born in New York City in 1930. While working as an art teacher in public

---

66. Faith Ringgold (2017). Biography. Available at https://www.biography.com/people/faith-ringgold-9459066.

schools, she began a series of paintings called *American People*, which portrayed the civil rights movement from a female perspective.

Figure 43. Painting from Faith Ringgold:
Free woman, free yourself.

In the 1970s, she created African-style masks, painted political posters, and actively sought the racial integration of the New York art world. During the 1980s, she began a series of quilts that are among her best-known works, and she later embarked on a successful career as a children's book author and illustrator. Faith Ringgold, born Faith Will Jones, was born on October 8, 1930, in the Harlem neighborhood of New York City.

She was the youngest of three children born to Andrew and Willi Jones, who raised their children during the Harlem Renaissance and exposed them to all of its cultural offerings. As she suffered from asthma as a young girl, Ringgold spent a great deal of time at home with her mother, a fashion designer who taught her to sew and work creatively with fabrics. Throughout her grammar and high school years, Ringgold also developed an interest in art and, by the time she graduated, became intent on turning her interest into a career.

Enrolling at the City College of New York in 1950, she wound up studying art education when the liberal arts department denied her application. That same year, she married musician Robert Wallace. In 1952, they had two daughters, one born in January and one born in December.

Faith and Robert would divorce several years later, when he developed a heroin addiction that would eventually lead to his death.

After receiving her bachelor's degree in fine art and education in 1955, Faith spent the latter half of the decade juggling several different roles. While looking after her children, she taught art in the public-school system and also enrolled in a graduate studies program at City College.

Ringgold began developing her own art, which at this time was fairly conventional. Faith received her master's degree in art in 1959 and later toured Europe, visiting many of its finest museums.

The early 1960s would prove to be a pivotal period for Faith.

She married Burdette Ringgold on May 19, 1962, and also embarked on creating a series of paintings—*American People*—that today rank among her most important work. Centered around themes from the civil rights movement, paintings such as *Neighbors*, *Die*, and *The Flag Is Bleeding* all capture the racial tensions of the era. Ringgold's first solo gallery show in 1967 featured the *American People* series.

Early into the 1970s, Ringgold's art took a new direction. She was deeply affected by her visit the Rijksmuseum in Amsterdam and its collection of Tibetan *thangka* paintings in particular. Upon returning to New York, Ringgold began to incorporate similar elements in her work, painting with acrylic on canvases with fabric borders and creating cloth dolls and soft sculptures, including *Wilt*, which depicted basketball legend Wilt Chamberlain.

After leaving her teaching job in 1973, Ringgold was free to focus on her art more. She began to pursue working in other mediums. She first branched out with a collection of portrait sculptures called *The Harlem Series* and then she created African-influenced masks that were included in performance pieces.

During this period, she also made posters in support of the Black Panthers and activist Angela Davis. After attempting unsuccessfully to have her autobiography published, at the turn of the decade Ringgold discovered a new way to tell her story. Once more drawing her inspiration from Tibetan art, and in honor of her mother's early influence, Ringgold began a series of quilts that are perhaps her best-known work.

She assembled the first quilt, *Echoes of Harlem*, in 1980 (a year before her mother passed away) and went on to make numerous others, eventually incorporating text as well. Among her narrative quilts are *Who's Afraid of Aunt Jemima* (1983), the Michael Jackson tribute *Who's Bad?* (1988), and her most famous offering, *Tar Beach, Part 1 from the Woman on the Bridge* series (1988), which is now part the Guggenheim Museum's permanent collection.

Meanwhile, Ringgold had become a professor of art at the University of California at San Diego, where she taught until 2002.

Displaying yet more talent, beginning in the 1990s, Ringgold embarked on a literary career, publishing the children's book *Tar Beach*, which she adapted from her quilt of the same name in 1991. In 1995, she published her memoir, *We Flew over the Bridge*; she has now written and illustrated more than fifteen other children's books. In recognition of her contributions as an artist and activist, Ringgold has received countless honors, including a National Endowment for the Arts Award, a Guggenheim Fellowship for painting, and an NAACP Image Award.

Percy Julian[67]

African American chemist Percy Julian was a pioneer in the chemical synthesis of medicinal drugs such as cortisone, steroids, and birth control pills. Born in Alabama in 1899, pioneering chemist Percy Julian was not allowed to attend high school but went on to earn his PhD. His research at academic and corporate institutions led to the chemical synthesis of drugs to treat glaucoma and arthritis, and although his race presented challenges at every turn, he is regarded as one of the most influential chemists in American history.

Percy Lavon Julian was born April 11, 1899, in Montgomery, Alabama, the grandson of former slaves. He attended school through

---

[67.] Percy Julian (2017). Biography. Available at https://www.biography.com/people/percy-julian-9359018.

the eighth grade, but there were no high schools open to black students. He applied to DePauw University in Greencastle, Indiana, where he had to take high school–level classes in the evening to get him up to the academic level of his peers.

In spite of this challenging beginning, he graduated first in his class, with Phi Beta Kappa honors. After college, Julian accepted a position as a chemistry instructor at Fisk University. He left in 1923 when he received a scholarship to attend Harvard University to finish his master's degree, though the university would not allow him to pursue his doctorate.

He traveled for several years, teaching at black colleges, before obtaining his PhD at the University of Vienna in Austria in 1931. With his doctorate in hand, he returned to DePauw to continue his research. In 1935, he earned international acclaim by synthesizing physostigmine from the calabar bean to create a drug treatment for glaucoma, but in spite of his success, the university refused to make him a full professor because of his race.

Desiring to leave academia, Julian applied for jobs at prominent chemical companies, but was repeatedly rejected when hiring managers discovered that he was black. Ultimately, he obtained a position at Glidden Company as the lab director. There he invented Aero-Foam, a product that uses soy protein to put out oil and gas fires and was widely used in World War II, as well as other soybean-based inventions.

Julian continued his biomedical work as well and discovered how to extract sterols from soybean oil and synthesize the hormones progesterone and testosterone. He was also lauded for his synthesis of cortisone, which became used in the treatment of rheumatoid arthritis. Julian left Glidden in 1953 and established his own laboratory, Julian Laboratories, in 1954.

He sold the company in 1961, becoming one of the first black millionaires, before founding Julian Research Institute, a nonprofit organization that he ran for the rest of his life. He died of liver cancer on April 19, 1975. Julian was the first black chemist elected to the National Academy of the Sciences in 1973.

In 1990, he was elected to the National Inventors Hall of Fame, and in 1999, his synthesis of physostigmine was recognized by the American Chemical Society as "one of the top twenty-five achievements in the history of American chemistry." Julian met his wife, Anna Roselle, while employed at Howard University, and the two were accused of having an affair while she was married to one of his colleagues. A scandal ensued and Julian was fired, but he and Anna married in 1935 and had two children.

Cesar Chavez[68]

Mexican American Cesar Chavez (figure 44) was a prominent union leader and labor organizer. Hardened by his early experience as a migrant worker, Chavez founded the National Farm Workers Association in 1962. His union joined with the Agricultural Workers Organizing Committee in its first strike against grape growers in California, and the two organizations later merged to become the United Farm Workers.

Figure 44. Cesar Chavez.

Stressing nonviolent methods, Chavez drew attention for his causes via boycotts, marches, and hunger strikes. Despite conflicts

---

68. Cesar Chavez (2017). History.com. Available at http://www.history.com/topics/cesar-chavez.

with the Teamsters union and legal barriers, he was able to secure raises and improve conditions for farm workers in California, Texas, Arizona, and Florida. Born in Yuma, Arizona, to immigrant parents, Chavez moved to California with his family in 1939.

For the next ten years, they moved up and down the state working in the fields. During this period, Chavez encountered the conditions that he would dedicate his life to changing: wretched migrant camps, corrupt labor contractors, meager wages for backbreaking work, bitter racism. His introduction to labor organizing began in 1952 when he met Father Donald McDonnell, an activist Catholic priest, and Fred Ross, an organizer with the Community Service Organization, who recruited Chavez to join his group.

Within a few years, Chavez had become national director, but in 1962 resigned to devote his energies to organizing a union for farm workers. A major turning point came in September 1965 when the fledgling Farm Workers Association voted to join a strike that had been initiated by Filipino farm workers in Delano's grape fields. Within months, Chavez and his union became nationally known.

Chavez's drawing on the imagery of the civil rights movement, his insistence on nonviolence, his reliance on volunteers from urban universities and religious organizations, his alliance with organized labor, and his use of mass mobilizing techniques such as a famous march on Sacramento in 1966 brought the grape strike and consumer boycott into the national consciousness. The boycott in particular was responsible for pressuring the growers to recognize the United Farm Workers (*ufw*, renamed after the union joined the *afl-cio*). The first contracts were signed in 1966, but were followed by more years of strife.

In 1968 Chavez went on a fast for twenty-five days to protest the increasing advocacy of violence within the union. Victory came finally on July 29, 1970, when twenty-six Delano growers formally signed contracts recognizing the *ufw* and bringing peace to the vineyards. That same year, the Teamsters' union challenged the *ufw* in the Salinas valley by signing sweetheart contracts with the growers there.

Thus began a bloody four-year struggle. Finally, in 1973, the Teamsters signed a jurisdictional agreement that temporarily ended the strife. Believing that the only permanent solution to the problems of farm workers lay in legislation, Chavez supported the passage of California's Agricultural Labor Relations Act (the first of its kind in the nation), which promised to end the cycle of misery and exploitation and ensure justice for the workers.

These promises, however, proved to be short-lived as grower opposition and a series of hostile governors undercut the effectiveness of the law. After 1976, Chavez led the union through a major reorganization, intended to improve efficiency and outreach to the public. In 1984, in response to the grape industry's refusal to control the use of pesticides on its crops, Chavez inaugurated an international boycott of table grapes. For thirty years, Chavez tenaciously devoted himself to the problems of some of the poorest workers in America. The movement he inspired succeeded in raising salaries and improving working conditions for farm workers in California, Texas, Arizona, and Florida.

Lynn Conway[69]

Lynn Conway is notable for her pivotal engineering achievements, which she attained during her time working at IBM. However, once she expressed her desire to transition to female, IBM fired her. In 2013, Conway and a colleague successfully lobbied the board of directors of the Institution of Electrical and Electronic Engineers, the world's largest engineering professional society, to include protections for transgender people in their code of ethics. In January 2014, the code became fully inclusive of LGBT people. That same year, *Time* magazine named Conway one of the "21 Transgender People Who Influenced American Culture."

[69.] Lynn Conway (2004). Lynn's Story. University of Michigan. Available at http://ai.eecs.umich.edu/people/conway/LynnsStory.html.

Lynn's Story[70]

Lynn Conway is a famed pioneer of microelectronics chip design. Her innovations during the 1970s at the Xerox Palo Alto Research Center (PARC) have impacted chip design worldwide. Many high-tech companies and computing methods have foundations in her work.

Thousands of chip designers learned their craft from Lynn's textbook Introduction to VLSI Systems, which she coauthored with Prof. Carver Mead of Caltech. Thousands more did their first VLSI design projects using the government's MOSIS prototyping system, which is based directly on Lynn's work at PARC. Much of the modern silicon chip design revolution is based on her work.

Lynn went on to win many awards and high honors, including election as a member of the National Academy of Engineering, the highest professional recognition an engineer can receive. What no one knew till recently is that Lynn also did earlier pioneering research at IBM in the 1960s. Fresh out of grad school, she invented a powerful method for issuing multiple out-of-order instructions per machine cycle in supercomputers.

By solving this fundamental computer architecture problem way back in 1965, she made possible the creation of the first true superscalar computer, and participated in its design at IBM. Lynn called her invention dynamic instruction scheduling (DIS). By the '90s, chips held enough transistors so that entire superscalar computers could be put on single chips.

Lynn's DIS invention suddenly became used in almost all the powerful new PC chips, making them much more powerful than they'd otherwise have been. Lynn's work thus had yet another big impact on the modern information technology revolution. Most computer engineers thought DIS was a generalization of decades of work, and had no idea it had been invented in 1965.

It caused Lynn great angst to see her wonderful invention so widely used, and described in all the computer architecture textbooks,

---

70. Ibid.

without anyone knowing it was her idea. How could this oversight have happened? Why did Lynn remain silent for over three decades about her IBM work?

The answer is that women like Lynn have lived, especially in the past, in a holocaust of stigmatization, persecution, and violence. They could not reveal their past identities without risking great physical danger to themselves, and great harm to their careers and their personal relationships. You see, Lynn was born and raised as a boy.

It was a terrible mistake, because Lynn had the brain-sex and gender identity of a girl. However, back in the forties and fifties there wasn't any knowledge about such things, and Lynn was forced to grow up as a boy. She did the best she could at it, but suffered terribly from what was happening to her.

She was still a boy and had a boy's name when she worked at IBM. After years and years of trying to find help, she finally connected with the pioneering physician Harry Benjamin, MD, in 1966, shortly after he'd published his seminal textbook *The Transsexual Phenomenon*. That text was the first to describe the true nature of, and medical solutions for, Lynn's mis-gendering affliction.

With Dr. Benjamin's help, Lynn began medical treatments in 1967. She became one of the very early transsexual women to undergo hormonal and surgical sex reassignment to have her body completely changed from that of a boy into that of a woman. Sadly, just before Lynn underwent sex reassignment surgery in 1968, she was fired by IBM for being transsexual and lost all connections to her important work there.

Lynn's case was a first at IBM. The idea that a professional person would seek a "sex change" totally shocked IBM's management. Most transsexual women seeking help back then were from among those who worked as female impersonators or as prostitutes.

Only those who were sure they could fully pass as women, who were totally desperate, and who had nothing to lose dared to change gender back then. When top IBM management learned what Lynn was doing, she was fired in a maelstrom of animosity. It is almost certain that the decision was made by T. J. Watson Jr. himself.

Lynn had managed to put together some fragile bits of support and help from her family and friends. However, when IBM fired her, everyone lost confidence in what she was doing and her support system collapsed. Lynn went abroad for her surgery all alone.

She had lost not only her career and professional reputation, but also her family, relatives, friends, and colleagues. She faced a frighteningly uncertain future without a soul in the world to help her other than her doctors. When Lynn returned, she made her social transition and took on her new name.

She started her career all over again as a lowly contract programmer without a past. A gritty survivor, her adjustment in her new role went completely against the dire predictions of the IBM executives and all the family and the friends who had deserted her. All alone she went out into the world, made new friends, and worked hard to succeed in her new life.

Amazingly, Lynn became so happy and so full of life and hope after her transformation that her career took off like a rocket. Moving up through a series of companies, she landed a computer architecture job at Memorex in 1971. In 1973, she was recruited by Xerox's exciting new Palo Alto Research Center, just as it was forming.

By 1978, just ten years after her gender transition, Lynn was already on the verge of international fame in her field for her VLSI innovations. By then she was writing the seminal textbook on the subject and was heading off to MIT to teach the first prototype course on VLSI systems. Within two years, universities all over the world were adopting her text for similar courses.

The Department of Defense started a major new program to sponsor research to build on her work. Scores of startup companies began incubating and forming to commercialize the knowledge. All this happened without people catching on to Lynn's secret past.

She could never have survived and done it if they had. In the '80s and '90s, Lynn went on to enjoy a wide-ranging, influential career and a wonderfully adventurous, fulfilling, and happy personal life. She is now professor of electrical engineering and computer science, Emerita, at the University of Michigan in Ann Arbor, where she also served for many years as associate dean of engineering.

She now lives on country property in rural Michigan with her husband, Charlie. They've been together since 1987. However, for thirty-one years after her transition, Lynn carefully remained in "stealth mode."

Only her closest friends knew about her past. Lynn knew of other transsexual women who had been socially ostracized, ghettoized, beaten, gang-raped, murdered, or driven to suicide when "read" or otherwise discovered by brutal, hateful people. For years Lynn lived with an ever-present sense of danger, fearful that exposure of her past could cause her to lose her civil rights, legal rights, and employment rights, and to suffer estrangements in her professional and personal relationships.

In 1999, computer historians finally stumbled into Lynn's early IBM work. They tracked it down to her, and her past was revealed among her colleagues. Frightened at first, she gradually realized times might have changed enough that she needn't be afraid to be "out" now.

She certainly has nothing at all to be ashamed of and is indeed very proud of the successes in her personal life as well as those in her career. At the same time, Lynn was dismayed that transsexual women are still treated so inhumanely by parents, relatives, employers, the legal system, and society at large. The total rejection of teenage transgender and transsexual girls-to-be by their families is especially tragic, since it often happens just as they first cry out for help and can doom them to years of marginalized existence.

Lynn began to think that her story might help somehow. Societal views are partly a media problem. Images of transsexualism routinely come from stories of "transition."

That's a time when media can focus on prurient, somewhat shocking, and often embarrassing aspects of someone's gender change. The stories seem superficially sympathetic, but often convey a sad, dreary image. Readers are left feeling sorry for the "poor things," and "certainly wouldn't want it to happen in their family."

What doesn't come through is the miracle of release from entrapment in a male body that the transsexual girl experiences and the happiness she finds as a woman later on. Folks never learn about the tens of thousands of post-operative women living among us who are very successful and fully accepted as regular gals. The public simply never sees these successes.

Why is this? Because almost all these women live in stealth, just as Lynn did, fearing what might happen if their pasts were revealed. Meanwhile, tens of thousands of young pre-operative transsexuals live in fear and doubt about their futures.

They are often excommunicated by their families and lose their jobs, as had happened to Lynn, when they identify their problem and seek medical help. Lynn is the first truly successful case to come out of long-term stealth and tell her story. That story should give hope to young transsexuals. It should help parents see possibilities for happiness for a transsexual daughter-to-be, especially if they were to support their child's efforts to transform a "boy's" body and become a woman early enough in life. It should also give employers pause for thought before firing someone just because of their transsexualism.

Dorothy Height[71]

Dorothy Height (figure 45) was a civil rights and women's rights activist focused primarily on improving the circumstances of and opportunities for African American women. Born in Virginia in 1912, Dorothy Height was a leader in addressing the rights of both women and African Americans as the president of the National Council of Negro Women. In the 1990s, she drew young people into her cause in the war against drugs, illiteracy, and unemployment.

[71.] Dorothy Height (2017). Biography. Available at https://www.biography.com/people/dorothy-height-40743.

Figure 45. Dorothy Height Library

The numerous honors bestowed upon her include the Presidential Medal of Freedom (1994) and the Congressional Gold Medal (2004). She died on April 20, 2010, in Washington, D.C. Dorothy Height spent her life fighting for civil rights and women's rights.

The daughter of a building contractor and a nurse, Height moved with her family to Rankin, Pennsylvania, in her youth. There, she attended racially integrated schools. In high school, Height showed great talent as an orator.

She also became socially and politically active, participating in anti-lynching campaigns. Height's skills as a speaker took her all the way to a national oratory competition. Winning the event, she was awarded a college scholarship.

Height had applied to and been accepted to Barnard College in New York, but as the start of school neared, the college changed its mind about her admittance, telling Height that they had already met their quota for black students. Undeterred, she applied to New York University, where she would earn two degrees: a bachelor's degree in education in 1930 and a master's degree in psychology in 1932. After working for a time as a social worker, Height joined the staff of the Harlem YWCA in 1937.

She had a life-changing encounter not long after starting work there. Height met educator and founder of the National Council of Negro Women Mary McLeod Bethune when Bethune and US first lady Eleanor Roosevelt came to visit her facility. Height soon volunteered with the NCNW and became close to McLeod.

One of Height's major accomplishments at the YWCA was directing the integration of all of its centers in 1946. She also established its Center for Racial Justice in 1965, which she ran until 1977. In 1957, Height became the president of the National Council of Negro Women.

Through the center and the council, she became one of the leading figures of the civil rights movement. Height worked with Martin Luther King Jr., A. Philip Randolph, Roy Wilkins, Whitney Young, John Lewis, and James Farmer—sometimes called the Big Six of the civil rights movement—on different campaigns and initiatives. In 1963, Height was one of the organizers of the famed March on Washington.

Height stood close to Martin Luther King Jr. when he delivered his "I Have a Dream" speech. Despite her skills as a speaker and a leader, Height was not invited to talk that day. Height later wrote that the March on Washington event had been an eye-opening experience for her.

Her male counterparts "were happy to include women in the human family, but there was no question as to who headed the household," she said, according to the *Los Angeles Times*. Height joined in the fight for women's rights. In 1971, she helped found the National Women's Political Caucus with Gloria Steinem, Betty Friedan, and Shirley Chisholm.

While she retired from the YWCA in 1977, Height continued to run the NCNW for two more decades. One of her later projects was focused on strengthening the African American family. In 1986, Height organized the first Black Family Reunion, a celebration of traditions and values which is still held annually.

In February 2017, the United States Postal Service issued a stamp honoring activist Dorothy Height in its Black Heritage series. Height received many honors for her contributions to society. In 1994, President Bill Clinton awarded her the Presidential Medal of Freedom.

She stepped down from the presidency of the NCNW in the late 1990s, but remained the organization's chair of the board until her death in 2010. In 2002, Height turned her nineti-eth birthday celebration into a fundraiser for the NCNW; Oprah Winfrey and Don King were among the celebrities who contributed to the event. In 2004, President George W. Bush gave Height the Congressional Gold Medal.

She later befriended the first African American president of the United States, Barack Obama, who called her "the godmother of the civil rights movement," according to the *New York Times*. Height died in Washington, D.C., on April 20, 2010. Former first lady and secretary of state Hillary Clinton was among the many who mourned the passing of the famed champion for equality and justice.

Clinton told the *Washington Post* that Height understood that women's rights and civil rights are indivisible. She stood up for the rights of women every chance she had. On February 1, 2017, the United States Postal Service kicked off Black History month with the issuance of the Dorothy Height Forever stamp (figure 57) honoring her civil rights legacy.

LaDonna Harris (Comanche)[72]

Since her Depression-era childhood in an Oklahoma dust bowl farm town, LaDonna Harris has been a crusader devoting her life to building coalitions that create change. As a result of her persistence to overcome opposition and success in creating positive change, the nationally renowned tribal advocate was honored with the *Spirit of*

---

[72]. La Donna Harris (2017). Indian Country Today. Available at https://indiancountrymedianetwork.com/news/comanche-with-a-cause-ladonna-harris-receives-spirit-of-the-heard-award/.

the Heard Award by the Heard Museum in Phoenix. In addition to recognizing the recipient's accolades as an individual and community leader, the award reinforces the mission of the museum itself: to educate the public about the heritage and living arts and cultures of Native peoples.

This recognition comes from LaDonna Harris's unparalleled career working for the cause of native peoples on a local, national, and international basis. The organization Harris founded, Americans for Indian Opportunity, has provided leadership training to hundreds of indigenous youth, many of whom are today's leaders across Indian Country. Harris is a tireless fighter for necessary policy change that serves as a catalyst for American Indian peoples.

She's an inspiration to all Native women not only through her defense of tribal rights, but also through her influence on civil rights and women's issues. Harris is no stranger to giving lectures in front of large audiences. She began her public service as the wife of US Senator Fred Harris and was the first senator's wife to testify before a congressional committee in the 1960s.

During that time, she founded Oklahomans for Indian Opportunity to find ways to reverse stifling socioeconomic conditions that impacted Indian communities. Harris has helped to start and build some of today's leading Indian organizations like the National Indian Business Association, National Tribal Environmental Council, National Indian Housing Council, and the Council of Energy Resource Tribes. In the mid-'90s, then Vice President Al Gore recognized her as a leader during a White House Tribal Summit.

Harris has been appointed to presidential commissions under four presidents: Jimmy Carter, Gerald Ford, Richard Nixon, and Lyndon Johnson. Since the 1970s, she has presided over Americans for Indian Opportunity, a group that catalyzes and facilitates culturally appropriate initiatives that enrich the lives of indigenous peoples. As a national leader over decades, Harris has influenced the agendas of several movements—civil rights, environmental, feminist, and world peace.

Grace Lee Boggs[73]

A prominent activist her entire adult life, Grace Lee was born in Rhode Island in 1915, the daughter of Chinese immigrants. She studied at Barnard College and Bryn Mawr, receiving her PhD in 1940. Her studies in philosophy and the writings of Marx, Hegel, and Margaret Mead led not to a life in academia, but rather to a lifetime of social activism.

Lee's activism began in Chicago, where she joined the movement for tenants' rights, and then the Workers Party, a splinter group of the Socialist Workers Party. In these associations, as well as in her involvement with the 1941 March on Washington, Lee focused on marginalized groups such as women and people of color. In 1953, Lee married black auto worker and activist James Boggs and moved to Detroit, where she remains an activist today, writing columns for the *Michigan Citizen*. James died in 1993.

Grace Lee Boggs embraces a philosophy of constant questioning—not just of who we are as individuals, but of how we relate to those in our community and country, to those in other countries, and to the local and global environment. Boggs has rejected the stereotypical radical idea that capitalist society is just something to be done away with, believing more that "you cannot change any society unless you take responsibility for it, unless you see yourself as belonging to it and responsible for changing it." She believes that it is by working together in small groups that positive social change can happen, not in large revolutions where one group of powers simply changes position with another.

With this philosophy, she and her husband founded Detroit Summer in 1992, a community movement bringing together people of all races, cultures, and ages to rebuild Detroit, a city Boggs has described as "a symbol of the end of industrial society . . . buildings that were once architectural marvels, like the Book Cadillac hotel and

---

[73.] Grace Lee Boggs (2017). Americans Who Tell the Truth. Available at https://www.americanswhotellthetruth.org/portraits/grace-lee-boggs.

Union Station, lie in ruins . . . and in most neighborhoods people live behind triple-locked doors and barred windows." Working from the ground up, Detroit Summer's activities include planting community gardens in vacant lots, creating huge murals on buildings, and renovating houses.

Kenneth Jernigan[74]

Dr. Kenneth Jernigan was a leader in the National Federation of the Blind for more than forty years. He was president from 1968 to 1977 and from 1978 to July 1986. Born in 1926, Kenneth Jernigan grew up on a farm in central Tennessee.

He received his elementary and secondary education at the school for the blind in Nashville. After high school, Jernigan managed a furniture shop in Beech Grove, Tennessee, making all furniture and operating the business. In the fall of 1945, Jernigan matriculated at Tennessee Technological University in Cookeville.

Active in campus affairs from the outset, he was soon elected to office in his class and to important positions in other student organizations. Jernigan graduated with honors in 1948 with a bachelor's degree in social science. In 1949, he received a master's degree in English from Peabody College in Nashville, where he subsequently completed additional graduate study.

While at Peabody, he was a staff writer for the school newspaper, cofounder of an independent literary magazine, and a member of the Writers Club. In 1949, he received the Captain Charles W. Browne Award, at that time presented annually by the American Foundation for the Blind to the nation's outstanding blind student. Jernigan then spent four years as a teacher of English at the Tennessee School for the Blind.

[74.] Dr. Kenneth Jernigan (2010). National Federation of the Blind. Available at http://www.blind.net/who-are-the-blind-who-lead-the-blind/dr-kenneth-jernigan-1926-to-1998.html.

During this period, he became active in the Tennessee Association of the Blind (now the National Federation of the Blind of Tennessee). He was elected to the vice presidency of the organization in 1950 and to the presidency in 1951. In that position, he planned the 1952 annual convention of the National Federation of the Blind, which was held in Nashville, and he has been planning national conventions for the Federation ever since.

It was in 1952 that Jernigan was first elected to the NFB board of directors. In 1953, he was appointed to the faculty of the California Orientation Center for the Blind in Oakland, where he played a major role in developing the best program of its kind then in existence. From 1958 until 1978, he served as director of the Iowa State Commission for the Blind.

In this capacity, he was responsible for administering state programs of rehabilitation, home teaching, home industries, an orientation and adjustment center, and library services for the blind and physically handicapped. The improvements made in services to the blind of Iowa under the Jernigan administration have never before or since been equaled anywhere in the country. In 1960, the federation presented Jernigan with its Newel Perry Award for outstanding accomplishment in services for the blind.

In 1968 Jernigan was given a special citation by the president of the United States. Harold Russell, the chairman of the president's Committee on Employment of the Handicapped, came to Des Moines to present the award. He said, "If a person must be blind, it is better to be blind in Iowa than anywhere else in the nation or in the world. This statement," the citation went on to say, "sums up the story of the Iowa Commission for the Blind during the Jernigan years and more pertinently of its director, Kenneth Jernigan. That narrative is much more than a success story. It is the story of high aspiration magnificently accomplished—of an impossible dream become reality."

Jernigan has received many honors and awards to enumerate individually, including honorary doctorates from three institutions of higher education. He has also been asked to serve as a special consultant to or member of numerous boards and advisory bodies.

The most notable among these are: member of the National Advisory Committee on Services for the Blind and Physically Handicapped (appointed by the Secretary of Health, Education, and Welfare), special consultant on Services for the Blind (appointed by the Federal Commissioner of Rehabilitation), advisor on museum programs for blind visitors to the Smithsonian Institution, and special advisor to the White House Conference on Library and Information Services (appointed by President Gerald Ford). Kenneth Jernigan's writings and speeches on blindness are better known and have touched more lives than those of any other individual writing today. On July 23, 1975, he spoke before the National Press Club in Washington, D.C., and his address was broadcast live throughout the nation on National Public Radio.

In 1978 Jernigan moved to Baltimore to become executive director of the American Brotherhood for the Blind and director of the National Center for the Blind. As president of the National Federation of the Blind at that time, he led the organization through the most impressive period of growth in its history. The creation and development of the National Center for the Blind and the expansion of the NFB into the position of being the most influential voice and force in the affairs of the blind stand as the culmination of Kenneth Jernigan's lifework and a tribute to his brilliance and commitment to the blind of this nation.

Speaking at a convention of the National Federation of the Blind, Jernigan said of the organization and its philosophy (and also of his own philosophy): "As we look ahead, the world holds more hope than gloom for us—and best of all, the future is in our own hands. For the first time in history we can be our own masters and do with our lives what we will; and the sighted—as they learn who we are and what we are—can and will work with us as equals and partners. In other words, we are capable of full membership in society, and the sighted are capable of accepting us as such—and for the most part, they want to.

"We want no Uncle Toms—no sellouts, no apologists, no rationalizers; but we also want no militant hell raisers or unbudging radicals. One will hurt our cause as much as the other. We must win true equality in society, but we must not dehumanize ourselves in the process; and we must not forget the graces and amenities, the compassions and courtesies which comprise civilization itself and distinguish people from animals and life from existence."

"Let people call us what they will and say what they please about our motives and our movement. There is only one way for the blind to achieve first-class citizenship and true equality. It must be done through collective action and concerted effort; and that means the National Federation of the Blind. There is no other way, and those who say otherwise are either uninformed or unwilling to face the facts. We are the strongest force in the affairs of the blind today, and we must also recognize the responsibilities of power and the fact that we must build a world that is worth living when the war is over—and for that matter, while we are fighting it. In short, we must use both love and a club, and we must have sense enough to know when to do which—long on compassion, short on hatred; and above all, not using our philosophy as a cop-out for cowardice or inaction or rationalization. We know who we are and what we must do—and we will never go back. The public is not against us. Our determination proclaims it; our gains confirm it; our humanity demands it."

William Moore[75]

In April of 1963, a Baltimore mailman set off to deliver the most important letter in his life—one he wrote himself. William Lewis Moore decided to walk along Highway 11 from Chattanooga, Tennessee, to Jackson, Mississippi, hoping to hand-deliver his letter to Gov. Ross Barnett. Moore wanted Barnett to fundamentally change Mississippi's racial hierarchy—something unthinkable for a Southern politician at the time.

In his letter, Moore warned the governor, "Do not go down in infamy as one who fought the democracy for all which you have not

[75.] Johnson, Miles (2013). A Postman's 1963 Walk For Justice, Cut Short On An Alabama Road. Available at http://www.npr.org/2013/08/14/211711898/a-postmans-1963-walk-for-justice-cut-short-on-an-alabama-road.

the power to prevent." It never reached its destination. Moore was shot on the roadside, a killer never charged.

Through time, Moore's story has been overshadowed by more emblematic moments that gripped the nation that year, like the assassination of civil rights leader Medgar Evers in Jackson, Mississippi, in May and the deaths of four black girls in the September bombing of the 16th Street Baptist Church in Birmingham, Alabama. But while Moore's walk for equality is less well-known, it's an important chapter in the civil rights movement for many.

William Moore was born in Binghamton, New York, but he was not just another "Yankee" sticking his nose where many Southerners believed it didn't belong. Moore had roots in the South. Moore was raised in Russell, Mississippi, after going to live with his grandparents at the age of two.

As an adult, Moore returned to Binghamton and began organizing demonstrations for civil rights. He also became a member of the Congress of Racial Equality (CORE) (figure 46), a vital arm of activism at the time. If you drove down Highway 11 five decades ago, you might have spotted a middle-aged white man in rumpled clothes and coiffed hair, sporting a gap-toothed grin.

Figure 46. CORE.

You might have thought little of it and kept driving. But when you glanced back, you would have wondered why this guy was pulling a little red wagon, handing letters to people he passed and pushing a grocery cart plastered with a "Wanted" poster featuring an image of Jesus. William Moore definitely stuck out.

But there were people along his route who did more than wonder about strangers like William Moore. Mary Stanton, author of *Freedom Walk*, a book about Moore and others who continued his effort after his death, describes people who confronted him. The polite individuals interrogated him about his intentions; the rude threatened him.

Ultimately, Moore was shot twice in the head at point-blank range near Attalla, Alabama. He was left on the side of the road at a picnic area approximately 300 miles short of Jackson. In her book, Stanton describes a frightened Willis Elrod, who stumbled over Moore's body when he pulled over to use the restroom.

Floyd Simpson, a Ku Klux Klan member, was suspected of committing the murder but was never charged. Today, the patch of dirt at that spot along Highway 11 is now only meaningful to those already aware of Moore's story; the stone picnic tables have long since been removed. Before April 23, 1963, they provided rest for travelers.

Afterward, they symbolized America's troubled past. But for some, that spot in Alabama inspired action. Decades after Moore's death, Ellen Johnson of Stanhope, New Jersey, decided the postman's story could not end at that picnic area.

In 2008, she and her friend Ken Loukinen set out to finish what Moore started. Johnson first learned about Moore's story while watching a film of Madalyn Murray O'Hair, an atheist activist, speaking to a group of law students. It's believed that Moore was an atheist and friend of O'Hair and that she helped make some of the signs he carried on his walk.

Once Johnson, also an atheist, learned that Moore was killed for his beliefs, she was determined to find and deliver his letter. Johnson located Moore's widow and obtained mimeographed copies that Moore was distributing on his march. On the forty-fifth anniversary of Moore's death, with copies of his letter in-hand, Johnson, Loukinen, and several others started their journey from the spot where Moore's body was found.

Johnson said that she noted at the time that not much of Alabama seemed changed since 1963. "There were some places, mostly Alabama, before we left Alabama, that looked like they hadn't changed in forty-five years," Johnson said. "Because it looked like I was seeing what Bill Moore saw."

But unlike Moore's journey fifty years ago, Johnson's walk to Jackson in 2008 garnered mild reactions. "I think they just wanted to know that we were okay and they moved on," Johnson said of travelers who passed them on the road. "Most people, eh, it was kind of ho-hum." For Johnson, completing this march was anything but "ho-hum."

Johnson said that honoring Moore and others was her goal. When the marchers arrived at Gov. Haley Barbour's office in 2008, he would not take time to accept the letter. Even so, there was a great sense of accomplishment among the marchers. Moore's letter remains undelivered, but Johnson takes pride in completing the postman's walk to Jackson. And though Moore never completed his own march to Mississippi, his values have since been delivered to more zip codes than he could have imagined.

Roman Ducksworth Jr. [76]

On April 9, 1962, Cpl. Roman Ducksworth Jr., a military police officer, was killed by Police Officer William Kelly. Ducksworth was traveling to Mississippi on an interstate bus from Forth Ritchie, Maryland, to visit his wife who was expecting their sixth child. There are two different accounts about the events leading up to Ducksworth's death.

[76.] Civil Rights and Restorative Justice (2017). Roman Ducksworth Jr.. Available at http://nuweb9.neu.edu/civilrights/mississippi/roman-duckworth-jr/.

The NAACP took on the case, reporting that Kelly shot Ducksworth after he refused Officer Kelly's order to move to the back of the bus. Ducksworth insisted that he had a right to sit where he chose on the bus. Ducksworth's brother gave a different account of the events.

According to Ducksworth's brother, when the bus arrived in Taylorsville, Mississippi, Ducksworth's hometown, Kelly came aboard the bus and awoke Ducksworth by hitting him. Officer Kelly ordered Ducksworth off the bus to beat him. Officer Kelly then shot Ducksworth in the heart.

According to this account, Kelly may have mistaken Ducksworth for a "freedom rider" because the bus traveled on the same roads as the freedom riders, who were hated in the area for testing bus desegregation laws. When Ducksworth died, he was a few months short of finishing ten years of service in the US army. Ducksworth's death shocked people who knew the Ducksworth family for their farming, church involvement, and support for the community. Ducksworth received full military honors and a sixteen-gun salute.

Legal Case[77]

There was never a trial connected with the Ducksworth shooting. A town marshal claimed Ducksworth was drunk, and a grand jury cleared Kelly days later, agreeing that he shot in self-defense. But fifty-one years later, Ducksworth's family members say they still are waiting for justice.

"There's something wrong with that story," Cordero Ducksworth told the *Huffington Post* of his father's death. "What reason did Kelly

---

[77.] Michael McLaughlin (2013). Roman Ducksworth Family Claims Department of Justice Overlooked Evidence in 1962 Killing. Available at http://www.huffingtonpost.com/2013/03/08/roman-ducksworth-death_n_2762916.html.

have to be afraid? [My father's] a human being. He's not just a human being, but he's a serviceman."

"He's a protector. It just doesn't look right." The Ducksworth family hoped to clear their father's name under the Emmett Till Unsolved Civil Rights Crime Act of 2007, which forced the Department of Justice and the FBI to reopen investigations into 112 racially motivated homicides, including Ducksworth's.

However, only one thus far has resulted in a conviction, according to a report from the US Attorney General's office last fall, and Ducksworth's, along with ninety other cases, were closed. But Cordero Ducksworth, fifty-six, said attorneys who volunteered to look at his father's case recently unearthed records showing segregationist informants for the notorious Mississippi State Sovereignty Commission had identified Ducksworth family members as "agitating" in their small town. When the DOJ closed the Ducksworth case in 2010, saying there was no one to prosecute, its final report didn't mention that the commission in 1958 had started monitoring some of Ducksworth's relatives who were believed to be NAACP activists.

"I want everything to be rewritten. I want my family to have closure and to know why that happened," said Ducksworth, who was five when his father died. "There's no reason why Mississippi should say this was justified."

Ducksworth's attorneys Janis McDonald and Paula Johnson, cofounders of Syracuse University's Cold Case Justice Initiative, uncovered files in February revealing that police stationed in and around Taylorsville passed along tips to the commission about Ducksworth's extended family. McDonald and Johnson said it's discouraging that federal agents looked past the trove of hundreds of thousands of pages of state snooping. They questioned the DOJ's effort to solve civil rights era murders as required by the Till Act.

"Unless you can push them and show them where their own documents are, they don't necessarily go and search," said McDonald. "You can never be quite sure that they've given you everything." The names of Ducksworth's relatives surfaced in the commission's files about NAACP activity in Taylorsville, which is about 60 miles southeast of Jackson.

Two highway patrolmen who were "very much opposed to integration," according to a March 3, 1959, memo to the commission's director, "claimed that the Negroes who were principally agitating at Taylorsville, Mississippi are named Duckworth." In Taylorsville, there are many people named Ducksworth and others named Duckworth. Cordero Ducksworth said they're all part of the same extended family.

At some point, some relatives dropped the "s." The names are also often misspelled. Many media accounts about Roman Ducksworth's shooting misidentified him as a Duckworth.

A shorter dispatch from March 2, 1959, said "some Negroes by the name of Duckworth were instigators of the NAACP in Taylorsville." A subsequent memo in the commission's archive from June 1959 said other members of law enforcement "mentioned the Duckworth Negroes and others who are already listed in our files who live around Taylorsville as possible members of the NAACP." Commission records aren't proof that Ducksworth's slaying was anything other than an isolated and legitimate use of force, but their absence from the DOJ's recent reinvestigation raises questions about the department's effort to dig up leads in the Ducksworth and other cold cases.

Tracking down every shred of decades-old evidence from sheriff's offices, district attorneys, state police, FBI bureaus, and the DOJ's civil rights division is a formidable challenge. Fires and floods destroy archives, and what survives can be lost by lackadaisical record keeping. Current investigators may never know if they've amassed a complete history.

Sovereignty commission documents, however, were released in 1998 as the result of an American Civil Liberties Union lawsuit and the Mississippi Department of Archives and History uploaded a searchable version to its website. The DOJ refused to discuss its investigation of the Ducksworth case with the *Huffington Post*, but released a statement saying it believed the Sovereignty Commission records are unrelated to the Ducksworth homicide. Once a determination is made that a matter is unprosecutable, the Department of Justice no longer has any authority to continue an investigation.

"Matters like the Duckworth case are unprosecutable, and therefore closed, because our investigation determined that the only subject is deceased. While we fully recognize that our mandate may leave some unanswered questions, we do not have the authority or resources to answer all the questions some may have that go beyond whether a case is prosecutable or not. And while we fully support those academics and members of the media who wish to learn more, our investigation must end when the relevant and necessary criminal evidence is obtained."

The 1962 shooting of Ducksworth immediately outraged many. News accounts said more than two thousand attended his funeral, a huge turnout in Taylorsville, population 1,132, according to the 1960 census. The army sent an integrated color guard to the ceremony for the fallen vet.

The NAACP showed *HuffPost* a copy of a telegram it wired to then President John F. Kennedy calling on him to "reassure the public conscience by making it unmistakably clear that you will enlist every appropriate measure at your command to see that Cpl. Duck[s] worth is brought to justice." The group also called for the Trailways bus driver to be fired, according to files in the NAACP's archive. Although it is possible that Ducksworth shooting was random, his death came at a time when civil rights activists and their families were frequent targets of conspiracies organized by members of law enforcement.

"That's why authorities should probe any possible connection between the informants who kept tabs on Ducksworth's relatives and his murder," said University of Southern Mississippi history professor Keven Greene. "It's extremely important knowing the paranoia of the Sovereignty Commission," Greene told *HuffPost*. "It's certainly worth digging into to see what can be found. It's a fascinating development."

No one in Ducksworth's family received a call or visit from a federal agent looking into the case while it was still open, Johnson told *HuffPost*. One day in 2010, a letter arrived for Ducksworth's widow telling her that the government had closed the investigation without prosecuting anyone. "We can't really point to much that happened to bring this or any of the cases to fruition," Johnson said."

Alvin Sykes, a Kansas City activist who lobbied for the Till Act, said the government has done a relatively good job investigating cold cases, considering the amount of time that had elapsed, and the age and reluctance of potential witnesses. "Given the depth of the atrocity and beginning so late," Sykes said, "it's been good and better than not anything at all." Kelly died in 2004, before the Till Act was passed.

Robert Parris Moses[78]

Robert Parris Moses was born in Harlem in 1935, the depth of the Great Depression. He was raised in a public housing project and worked in a black-owned milk cooperative as a young boy, and had both Christian and pan-Africanist influences in his extended family upbringing. His grandfather was a respected progressive Baptist clergyman and former black college president, an uncle headed a branch of the NAACP, aunts were militant defenders of black rights, race and politics were continuous topics of conversation at home.

His mother was a strong woman, a high school graduate who'd planned to go to college before marriage took her in a family direction. His father involved him in political conversations, always emphasizing the "little guy," and taught him how to read people by listening and paying careful attention to them. This upbringing influenced Bob Moses's perspective on non-institutional Christianity; Quaker pacifism, Gandhian nonviolence; reaction to the paternalism and often thinly disguised prejudice of predominantly white, liberal

---

[78]. Mike Miller (2016). The Organizer's Organizer: Bob Moses and the Fight for Voting Rights. Available at https://www.dissentmagazine.org/online_articles/voting-rights-organizer-bob-moses-laura-visser-maessen-biography-review.

private schools, colleges, and individuals; the political left; linguist Ludwig Wittgenstein; and most of all, Camus's existentialism.

In the early 1960s, Moses met Bayard Rustin, Pete Seeger, Allard Lowenstein, and other figures who would later become allies in his Mississippi work. Moses was an excellent student, a good athlete and campus leader, and at the same time, a reserved and quiet person. In 1960, he heard Martin Luther King Jr.'s aide Wyatt T. Walker extol King's leadership and emphasize the importance of following him.

After the talk, Moses said to Walker, "Don't you think we need a lot of leaders?" Later that year, Moses went south; he met students engaged in Atlanta's sit-in movement.

At first, the students viewed him suspiciously. He was different from them in many ways: older, northern, Harvard-educated, well-traveled internationally, and familiar with left ideologies. Some of them thought he might be a communist. They watched him carefully.

But he did grunt work—putting out mailings and daily manning a picket line, among other things—that impressed them. And he didn't try to impose any of his beliefs on them. At the time Moses arrived in Atlanta, SNCC was planning a conference to broaden its base of student affiliates.

There were few attendees from Deep South states. Moses said he'd take a trip to identify and invite people and see what was happening in the field. Ella Baker, a largely unsung heroine of the civil rights movement, gave him a list of contacts—black activists making up an informal network seeking to break racism's iron grip on the region.

At the end of his trip, he submitted to SNCC a list of some two hundred names. Jane Stembridge, a white Southerner who was SNCC's first full-time employee (she ran the SNCC office in Atlanta) and Moses's contact person during the trip, was deeply impressed. So were others.

Moses's quiet, persistent, competent, and thoughtful work was gaining a reputation. From Ella Baker, Moses (figure 71) learned an elaborated view of grassroots organizing. Her aphorism, "strong people don't need strong leaders," would become a SNCC theme.

Among the strong people Moses met on his trip was Amzie Moore. A veteran of the Second World War who had become an independent businessman in the Mississippi Delta, Moore was looking for a way to break voting barriers that resulted in almost no black voter participation in towns, counties, and the second congressional district of the state, where blacks were a majority of the population. Moore took Moses in and made him family. Moses was persuaded by Moore's argument that voter registration, not public accommodation desegregation or school integration, was the key to black freedom.

They devised a program in which SNCC would send a substantial force of full-time workers into the Delta to engage its black majority in politics. This was the beginning of SNCC's transformation from a coordinating committee of campus-based groups to a cadre of full-time workers, some of whom became organizers. Moore and Moses decided that the first voter registration project should be in minority-black southwest Mississippi, not the majority-black plantation region of the Delta.

Moses worked judiciously with existing leaders in McComb, as well as their own investment—money (local funding for the project was substantial). After being jailed on a phony charge, Moses used a contact in the Department of Justice Civil Rights Division to secure his release. Moses later called the 1957 Civil Rights Act's protection afforded voting rights workers a "crawl space" that made it possible for SNCC to continue its work.

Without it, he said in later years, the activists would have rotted in jail. During this period, Moses confronted fear and nonviolently responded to physical attacks: "I learned to live with my fears . . . [you just] pick one foot up and step forward, put it down and pick the next one up . . . [you learn] the importance of daily routine carrying you through. . . . The question of personal fear just has to be constantly fought. . . . [It's] an inside question [to which] I don't know if there is any answer at all."

It was in Amite County, a black-majority county with just one black voter registered when SNCC arrived, that Moses (figure 72) had to deal with deaths that resulted from the civil rights movement's work. First, in September 1961, Herbert Lee, a courageous local farmer engaged in the voter registration efforts, was shot in cold blood by a white neighbor and childhood friend who was also a local politician. Then, in January 1964, Louis Allen was murdered when the FBI leaked to local whites that he would give testimony at the grand jury hearing that challenged the official "self-defense" argument used by Lee's killer.

The deaths, along with other difficulties, put a chill on action in southwest Mississippi; the action moved to the Delta. Moses's overriding commitments were two: build SNCC as an organization of organizers—particularly young African Americans from Mississippi and the rest of the Deep South—and build black people-power vehicles in the state. By 1963, however, it was evident that without a change in tactics, Mississippi black lives would continue not to matter—not to the local power structure, the federal government, the national news media, or to white America.

That realization set in motion a number of decisions, the most important of which was to bring the country to Mississippi in the person of mostly white volunteers. The first foray in this direction was the Freedom Vote, a parallel election held in protected spaces in the black community: churches, barbershops, beauty salons, restaurants, and elsewhere. Some eighty-three thousand African Americans cast ballots, clearly demonstrating their interest in becoming equal citizens.

Dozens of white student volunteers from Yale and Stanford brought the nation's news media with them. The National Council of Churches brought hundreds of clergymen—Catholics, Protestants, and Jews—to Hattiesburg to participate in a voter registration support day. The media came again.

The Freedom Vote's success prompted bolder plans for what now is remembered as the 1964 Mississippi Freedom Summer, when more than eight hundred mostly white, northern students from mostly middle-class and elite families were recruited to participate in various programs in the black community. Early in the project, two volunteers and a local activist were murdered in a conspiratorial act that involved the Ku Klux Klan and local sheriff. A national outcry ensued.

President Lyndon Johnson ordered US military personnel into the state to dredge rivers and dig up suspicious sites to find them. Mississippi's governor claimed the three missing people were in hiding, and that it was all a trick to gain sympathy for communist agitators. As federal troops combed the state, they found the bodies of black Mississippians who had been lynched earlier.

Mainstream media and politicians accused SNCC of provoking violence for its own nefarious ends before the three organizers' bodies were finally found two months later. Freedom schools, community centers, and health screenings were all part of the summer effort. But its central focus was voter registration and the development of the Mississippi Freedom Democratic Party (MFDP), organized to challenge the white "regulars" who made up the state's official Democratic Party at the August 1964 Democratic Party Convention.

In a bitter struggle that revealed President Lyndon Johnson's determination to keep an insurgent black-led party out of his Democratic Party, MFDP (figure 74) lost. The summer's activities took place as if in a cyclone. Two rules of power operated against MFDP: first, when you borrow someone else's power (in this case the national liberal-labor-civil rights organizations), if your and their interests diverge, theirs will prevail.

Second, it is short-term, not long-term, interests that typically determine political decisions and outcomes. When Lyndon Johnson turned the screws on his liberal and labor allies, they capitulated and abandoned their initial support for the MFDP challenge. Typically, major defeats lead to disarray and conflict among the defeated as they seek to explain why their anticipated victory was not realized.

Many movement workers suffered deep fatigue and burnout; psychiatrist Robert Coles said it was "a state of mind comparable to shellshock or posttraumatic stress disorder." Noted African American psychiatrist Alvin Poussaint, a careful student of racism's impact on black mental health, was astounded at the psychological impact of Mississippi civil rights workers' continuous exposure to danger. The energy that was devoted to organizing and politics took new forms, many of them some version of dropping out.

In SNCC, militant rhetoric and slogans, African-influenced personal styling (dress and hair), and distancing from whites increasingly characterized the organization. Countercultural politics took the place of alternative institutions like the MFDP, freedom schools, and community centers. For others, things got worse: depression, alcoholism, drug addiction.

Lives of quiet despair sometimes exploded years later, as when former Freedom Summer volunteer Dennis Sweeney murdered his one-time hero, former liberal congressman, and Mississippi movement supporter Allard Lowenstein. The people with whom Bob Moses initially worked in Mississippi epitomized Ella Baker's "strong people." Independent black businesspeople, farmers, and sleeping car porters all worked in relatively autonomous circumstances.

The self-employed businessperson's market was the black community, which provided insulation from the white power structure. The sleeping car porters had the protection of an African American–led union; their travels took them out of the South and exposed them to places where greater freedom existed. The independent farmers overcame extraordinary obstacles simply to survive.

The Robert Parris Moses era ended in 1967, when it was becoming safe for black citizens to engage in politics. Soon, the black church, black teachers, and other more cautious black people and their cautious organizations were entering politics. Ella Baker's and Bob Moses's "strong people" were not able to withstand their conservatizing presence because their base in the black community didn't go deep enough. The old MFDP was marginalized. Only in a few places did it have the depth of popular support to withstand the cooptation that became the national Democratic Party's modus operandi in Mississippi after the 1964 convention.

Mamie Till Bradley[79]

Mamie Till Bradley, advocate for racial justice, was born Mamie Elizabeth Carthan. Her father, Wiley Nash Carthan, was a factory worker; her mother, the former Alma Spearman, had been a domestic. Mamie Carthan was born in Webb, Mississippi, a hamlet near the Tallahatchie County seat of Sumner, and was raised in Argo, a suburb of Chicago, where she graduated high school.

In 1940, at the age of eighteen, Carthan married Louis Till. Their only child, Emmett Louis, nicknamed "Bobo," was born a year later, on July 25. The couple separated not long afterward and Louis Till joined the US army in 1942 and served in Italy.

On 2 July 1945, the military hanged him for the murder of an Italian woman and the rape of two others (though the pervasiveness of racial prejudice casts doubt on his guilt). Mamie Till worked as a clerk typist at an aeronautics school, and she married Pink Bradley in 1951. After living briefly in Detroit, Mamie Till Bradley and her husband moved back to Chicago, where the marriage had effectively ended by the beginning of 1953.

Emmett grew into a lively and good-natured child, a snappy dresser who was popular with other children. Possibly because of a bout with polio, he suffered from a speech defect. Bobo was scheduled to enter the eighth grade when his mother reluctantly acceded to his request to visit his cousins in the Mississippi Delta.

Emmett left Chicago on August 20 to stay with his mother's uncle, Moses Wright, and his wife, Elizabeth. Their farm was about three miles from Money, Mississippi, where Emmett went on August 24 to buy two cents' worth of bubble gum at Bryant's Grocery Store and Meat Market. What else happened there is subject to conflicting accounts, uncertain memories, and conjecture.

[79.] Stephen J. Whitfield. "Bradley, Mamie Till"; Available at http://www.anb.org/articles/15/15-01388.html American National Biography Online October 2015 Update.

But presumably as a prank, Bobo wolf-whistled at the twenty-one-year-old wife of the proprietor, Carolyn Bryant. Four nights later, in the dark early hours that Sunday, her husband, Roy, and his half-brother, J. W. Milam, dragged "the boy from Chicago" from the Wright home and drove him to Sunflower County, where Emmett Louis Till was beaten and killed. Weighted down with a cotton gin fan that had been tied around his neck with several feet of barbed wire, his body was dumped in the Tallahatchie River.

A gruesomely bloated corpse was soon discovered, and Milam and Bryant were charged with kidnapping and murder. State authorities had intended a quick burial in their state. But the grieving Mamie Till Bradley ensured that her son's death would become an international incident by refusing to allow Emmett to be buried in Mississippi.

She insisted not only that the corpse be returned home, but also that an open casket be provided at the funeral home to which his disfigured body had been sent. She wanted "the whole world to see what they did to my boy." Over the course of four days, tens of thousands of mourners walked past the casket, and the shock was amplified in black communities when *Jet* magazine put on its September 15 cover his unrecognizable face.

The denunciation that the executive secretary of the National Association for the Advancement of Colored People (NAACP), Roy Wilkins, issued was scathing: "The State of Mississippi has decided to maintain white supremacy by murdering children." Novelist William Faulkner, a native Mississippian, struck an apocalyptic note by asserting that, if children are murdered for such a reason and in such fashion, Americans "don't deserve to survive, and probably won't." In September, Mamie Till Bradley entered the humid courthouse in Sumner to testify that the body was indeed her son's; he had been wearing his father's ring, which she also identified.

Though she had earlier vowed that "someone is going to pay for this. The entire state of Mississippi is going to pay," in the short run, her prediction was false. All five attorneys who were practicing in Sumner represented the defendants pro bono, and a jury consisting of twelve white men barely deliberated before acquitting the half-brothers.

Not even the presence of the media from elsewhere in the nation as well as abroad, plus the black press, seemed to nick the laws and customs of what its champions called "the Southern way of life." Early in 1956 in *Look* magazine, Milam and Bryant even confessed to the murder. But because of the prohibition against double jeopardy, they remained immune to further prosecution.

The case nevertheless gnawed at the nation's conscience. Perhaps it was due to Emmett Till's youth, as well as the wildly exaggerated fears of miscegenation stemming from a mere whistle. Whatever progress the South might claim in moderating its segregationist policies and customs suffered a setback when a fourteen-year-old visitor encountered a white woman in Mississippi.

He thus inadvertently exposed the violence of the Deep South's devotion to white supremacy, even as the Cold War was compelling the US government to court the favor of the Third World. Because of this international context and Mamie Till Bradley's decision to force the issue with an open-casket funeral, Emmett Till's death would not be confined to obscurity. Indeed, Rosa Parks later testified that she had his fate in mind when, three months later, she resolved to defy the law compelling blacks to be seated from the rear while riding buses in Montgomery, Alabama.

Younger black Southerners grasped the precariousness of their own lives, and later cited Till's murder as motivating them, during the following decade, to participate in the civil rights movement. Its climactic moment came with the March on Washington, which represented "progress," his mother later reflected in her autobiography. "But it was progress . . . that came at great cost."

Though she did not attend the march, she watched it on television, eight years to the day of Emmett Till's death. By 1957 she had remarried, this time happily. Her third husband was Gennie Mobley, who worked as a barber and also in a factory of the Ford Motor Company.

Though she had done clerical work for the Social Security Administration and then for the US Air Force, the loss of her son devastated her, and it inspired her to work with children. Till-Mobley studied at Chicago Teachers College, graduating in 1960; she began teaching in an elementary school soon thereafter. She also organized groups of black children who were taught to recite speeches that marked the struggle for racial justice, and beginning in 1973, these teams called themselves the Emmett Till Players.

Till-Mobley also earned a master's degree in administration from Loyola University of Chicago, before retiring from teaching in 1983. She lived to see the establishment of memorials in such cities as Denver and Montgomery, and to walk on the street that Chicago named for her son. "I realized," Mamie Till-Mobley wrote in her autobiography, "that Emmett had achieved the significant impact in death that he had been denied in life." Having converted her private grief into a public life, she died in Chicago.

Ruby Bridges[80]

Ruby Bridges was the first African American child to attend an all-white public elementary school in the American South. Born on September 8, 1954, in Tylertown, Mississippi, Ruby Bridges was six when she became the first African American child to integrate a white Southern elementary school, having to be escorted to class by her mother and US marshals due to violent mobs. Bridges's bravery paved the way for continued civil rights action and she's shared her story with future generations in educational forums.

Early Life

Ruby Nell Bridges was born on September 8, 1954, in Tylertown, Mississippi, and grew up on the farm her parents and grandparents sharecropped in Mississippi. When she was four years

---

[80]. Ruby Bridges (2017). Biography. Available at https://www.biography.com/people/ruby-bridges-475426

old, her parents, Abon and Lucille Bridges, moved to New Orleans, hoping for a better life in a bigger city. Her father got a job as a gas station attendant and her mother took night jobs to help support their growing family.

Soon, young Ruby had two younger brothers and a younger sister. The fact that Ruby Bridges was born the same year that the Supreme Court's Brown v. Board of Education decision desegregated the schools is a notable coincidence in her early journey into civil rights activism. When Ruby was in kindergarten, she was one of many African American students in New Orleans who were chosen to take a test determining whether she could attend a white school.

It is said the test was written to be especially difficult so that students would have a hard time passing. The idea was that if all the African American children failed the test, New Orleans schools might be able to stay segregated for a while longer. Ruby lived a mere five blocks from an all-white school, but attended kindergarten several miles away, at an all-black segregated school.

Her father was averse to his daughter taking the test, believing that if she passed and was allowed to go to the white school, there would be trouble. Her mother, Lucille, however, pressed the issue, believing that Ruby would get a better education at a white school. She was eventually able to convince Ruby's father to let her take the test.

Escorted by Federal Marshals

In 1960, Ruby Bridges's parents were informed by officials from the NAACP that she was one of only six African American students to pass the test. Ruby would be the only African American student to attend the William Frantz School, near her home, and the first black child to attend an all-white elementary school in the South. When the first day of school rolled around in September, Ruby was still at her old school.

All through the summer and early fall, the Louisiana State Legislature had found ways to fight the federal court order and slow the integration process. After exhausting all stalling tactics, the legislature had to relent, and the designated schools were to be integrated that November. Fearing there might be some civil disturbances, the federal district court judge requested the US government to send federal marshals to New Orleans to protect the children.

On the morning of November 14, 1960, federal marshals drove Ruby and her mother five blocks to her new school. While in the car, one of the men explained that when they arrived at the school, two marshals would walk in front of Ruby and two would be behind her. The image of this small black girl being escorted to school by four large white men inspired Norman Rockwell to create the painting *The Problem We All Must Live With*, which graced the cover of *Look* magazine in 1964.

When Ruby and the federal marshals arrived at the school, large crowds of people were gathered in front yelling and throwing objects. There were barricades set up, and policemen were everywhere. Ruby, in her innocence, first believed it was like a Mardi Gras celebration. When she entered the school under the protection of the federal marshals, she was immediately escorted to the principal's office and spent the entire day there. The chaos outside, and the fact that nearly all the white parents at the school had kept their children home, meant classes weren't going to be held.

Ostracized at School

On her second day, the circumstances were much the same as the first, and for a while, it looked like Ruby Bridges wouldn't be able to attend class. Only one teacher, Barbara Henry, agreed to teach Ruby. She was from Boston and a new teacher to the school.

Mrs. Henry, as Ruby would call her even as an adult, greeted her with open arms. Ruby was the only student in Henry's class, because parents pulled or threatened to pull their children from Ruby's class and send them to other schools. For a full year, Henry and Ruby sat side by side at two desks, working on Ruby's lessons.

Henry was very loving and supportive of Ruby, helping her not only with her studies, but also with the difficult experience of being ostracized. Ruby Bridges's first few weeks at Frantz School were not easy ones. Several times she was confronted with blatant racism in full view of her federal escorts.

On her second day of school, a woman threatened to poison her. After this, the federal marshals allowed her to only eat food from home. On another day, she was "greeted" by a woman displaying a black doll in a wooden coffin.

Ruby's mother kept encouraging her to be strong and pray while entering the school, which Ruby discovered reduced the vehemence of the insults yelled at her and gave her courage. She spent her entire day, every day, in Mrs. Henry's classroom, not allowed to go to the cafeteria or out to recess to be with other students in the school. When she had to go to the restroom, the federal marshals walked her down the hall.

Several years later, federal marshal Charles Burks, one of her escorts, commented with some pride that Ruby showed a lot of courage. She never cried or whimpered, Burks said, "She just marched along like a little soldier."

Effect on the Bridges Family

The abuse wasn't limited to only Ruby Bridges; her family suffered as well. Her father lost his job at the filling station, and her grandparents were sent off the land they had sharecropped for over twenty-five years. The grocery store where the family shopped banned them from entering.

However, many others in the community, both black and white, began to show support in a variety of ways. Gradually, many families began to send their children back to the school and the protests and civil disturbances seemed to subside as the year went on. A neighbor provided Ruby's father with a job, while others volunteered to babysit the four children, watch the house as protectors, and walk behind the federal marshals on the trips to school.

After winter break, Ruby began to show signs of stress. She experienced nightmares and would wake her mother in the middle of the night seeking comfort. For a time, she stopped eating lunch in her classroom, which she usually ate alone.

Wanting to be with the other students, she would not eat the sandwiches her mother packed for her, but instead hid them in a storage cabinet in the classroom. Soon, a janitor discovered the mice and cockroaches who had found the sandwiches. The incident led Mrs. Henry to lunch with Ruby in the classroom.

Ruby started seeing child psychologist Dr. Robert Coles, who volunteered to provide counseling during her first year at Frantz School. He was very concerned about how such a young girl would handle the pressure. He saw Ruby once a week either at school or at her home.

During these sessions, he would just let her talk about what she was experiencing. Sometimes his wife came too, and like Dr. Coles, she was very caring toward Ruby. Coles later wrote a series of articles for *Atlantic Monthly* and eventually a series of books on how children handle change, including a children's book on Ruby's experience.

Overcoming Obstacles

Near the end of the first year, things began to settle down. A few white children in Ruby's grade returned to the school. Occasionally, Ruby got a chance to visit with them.

By her own recollection many years later, Ruby was not that aware of the extent of the racism that erupted over her attending the school. But when another child rejected Ruby's friendship because of her race, she began to slowly understand. By Ruby's second year at Frantz School, it seemed everything had changed.

Mrs. Henry's contract wasn't renewed, and so she and her husband returned to Boston. There were also no more federal marshals; Ruby walked to school every day by herself. There were other students in her second-grade class, and the school began to see full enrollment again.

No one talked about the past year. It seemed everyone wanted to put the experience behind them. Ruby Bridges finished grade school and graduated from the integrated Francis T. Nicholls High School in New Orleans. She then studied travel and tourism at the Kansas City business school and worked for American Express as a world travel agent. In 1984, Ruby married Malcolm Hall in New Orleans and later became a full-time parent to their four sons.

Recent Contributions

In 1993, Ruby Bridges's youngest brother, Malcolm Bridges, was murdered in a drug-related killing. For a time, Ruby looked after Malcolm's four children, who attended William Frantz School. She began to volunteer at the school three days a week and soon became a parent-community liaison.

The coincidence of all this, to have her brother's death bring her back to her elementary school where so much had taken place, didn't escape Ruby, but she wasn't sure why all this happened. In 1995, she got her answer. Robert Coles, Bridges's child psychologist, published a children's book on his time with her, entitled *The Story of Ruby Bridges*. Soon after, Barbara Henry, her teacher that first year at Frantz School, contacted Bridges and they were reunited on *The Oprah Winfrey Show*.

Lt. Col. Lemuel Penn[81]

The eyes of the nation turned to Madison County fifty years ago July 11 when Lt. Col. Lemuel Penn, a black WWII veteran, was murdered in the night by the Ku Klux Klan (figure 48). The killing came just nine days after the passage of the Civil Rights Act on July 2, 1964. That legislation officially ended the Jim Crow era

---

[81.] Zach Mitcham (2014). On Race and Justice: A look back at the murder of Lemuel Penn. Available at http://www.madisonjournaltoday.com/archives/7060-On-Race-and-Justice-A-look-back-at-the-murder-of-Lemuel-Penn.html.

of "separate but equal" by prohibiting racial discrimination in the workplace or at any accommodations or facilities open to the public.

But ink on a page in a federal building was one thing. Implementing such an act was an entirely different matter— not a legislative one, but a battle of the soul in a racially divisive society. There was resistance. There was violence.

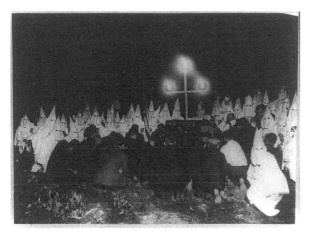

Figure 47. Ku Klux Klan

In the early morning hours of July 11, 1964, two shotgun blasts ripped through the rural quiet of Madison County, claiming the life of Penn, a forty-nine-year-old black man, a World War II veteran, a husband and a father of three, who supervised five vocational schools in Washington, D.C., while also being an active church member and Boy Scout leader, who had organized a scout camp for under-privileged black youth. The federal government responded in force, sending dozens of investigators to northeast Georgia. The case became a test of the equal rights issue.

If there was no justice for a distinguished black educator and war veteran murdered in the night as he drove home from reserve duty to his family, would the Civil Rights Act hold up against the resistance? The nation watched as the courtroom in Danielsville filled in August. Two men, Cecil Myers and Howard Sims, both known Ku Klux Klan members, would stand trial for killing Penn.

Taking It All In

They were accused of following him from Athens, then firing at him with double-barreled, sawed-off shotguns as they sped by in a car driven by James Lackey on Highway 172 at the Broad River Bridge at the Madison-Elbert County line. Boyd Jordan was the man assigned to transcribe it all as a court reporter. He entered the Madison County courtroom August 31, 1964, the first day of the trial, carrying a new podium, which stayed in the courtroom "until just a few years ago."

He then took his place at his shorthand machine and watched as a crowd flocked in, many of them, "perhaps seventy-five to a hundred," were reporters from state and national publications. Jordan, who was interviewed by this newspaper about the Penn case in 2004, had been at the job for less than two years at the time of the Penn case. Despite the national attention, Jordan wasn't nervous.

"I'd been at it long enough to where it [the attention] didn't bother me," said Jordan in the 2004 interview. The judge for the trial was Carey Skelton, a World War II colonel and former prosecutor, whom Jordan recalled as a "nice, distinguished gentleman."

"He was the most patriotic man I ever met," said Jordan, adding that when he first began working for Skelton, the judge sometimes had him call President John F. Kennedy.

A Judge's Perspective

Jordan remembered that he would call up the White House, get the president's secretary, leave a message that Judge Skelton wanted to speak with President Kennedy, then the phone would ring later with the secretary saying that President Kennedy was on the line for Judge Skelton. The Sunday before the August term of the Madison County Grand Jury, in which Myers and Sims would be indicted for the Penn murder, Skelton called Jordan and asked him to come in to work. It was one week before the murder trial and Skelton wanted Jordan to type out his charge to the grand jury.

The court reporter didn't leave until 3 a.m. Monday. "I typed it at least ten times," said Jordan. "He just could never get it to say what he wanted."

Skelton's twenty-seven-page grand jury charge outlined what was required of jurors, including the setting aside of any prejudice. "The court is a forum wherein all of the rights of all our citizens; whether they be rich or poor, no matter what their station in life is, whether they be white or black, red or yellow, the deliberation of the jury, both traverse and grand jury, should be calmly considered and determined, gentlemen, according to the established rules of law . . .," said Skelton.

While the judge offered advice to the jury, he seemed to be speaking to a larger audience too, offering views that America "has gone to sleep," that the country needs to be vigilant in combating the "twin evils" of "communism and atheism." He also spoke against civil rights legislation. "These Northern politicians in the United States Senate, they are just going to cram it down our throats," he stated.

The judge maintained that the push for civil rights legislation pitted property rights against privileges, noting that a man has a right to say who can come into his place of business or who he can hire, but "there is no true right that a man be accepted as a customer, it is, at best, a privilege." He maintained that in passing the civil rights legislation, the federal government was ushering in a police state, by interfering with the rights of business owners to welcome or exclude whomever they chose. He told the grand jury that such actions by the federal government would be a step toward communism and would "be the beginning of the end of freedom in this country."

Witnessing the Murder

Following jury selection in which the only two potential black jurors were stricken from consideration by the defense team, the prosecution opened its case by presenting firsthand accounts of a night of terror. They called their first two witnesses, Charles Brown and John Howard, Penn's fellow reserve officers who were in the car with the victim the night he was killed. Penn, Brown, and Howard had served a two-week stint in army reserve training at Ft. Benning, near Columbus.

They left immediately after their training officially ended at midnight, July 11, ready to get back to their families and their regular routines in Washington. The three traveled in Brown's Chevrolet Sedan, stopping in Atlanta to get gas, then stopping again in Athens when Brown became too sleepy to drive. Penn took the wheel and Brown fell asleep in the passenger seat.

Earlier, the group looked at a map and agreed to take a shortcut through Madison County, taking Highway 72 east, then Highway 172 north. Brown testified that he later awoke to two loud blasts, first thinking the car's tires had blown. The vehicle was out of control, and both Brown and Howard, who was in the backseat, lunged for the steering wheel.

Brown felt something hot on his left arm, which he later discovered was Penn's blood. And the car slammed into the side of the Broad River Bridge before they could stop the vehicle. "As soon as I could get his [Penn's] foot off the brakes and accelerator, we did stop the car, which was on the other side of the bridge," Brown said, according to the trial transcript.

Brown had seen two lights disappear into the fog ahead, but Howard had been awake at the time of the shooting and testified that he saw a cream-colored '61 or '62 Chevrolet. He couldn't tell who was in the vehicle but believed he saw "three or four" silhouettes. Their friend was dead. And they feared they might soon face the same fate. Howard had "observed light shadows as if they were going in a counterclockwise direction" and believed that the shooters were turning around. Brown moved his friend, vocational school supervisor and bridge partner, now slain, aside so that he could take the wheel.

He turned the car around and sped back toward Athens in the fog on an unfamiliar road, with a dead friend of over twenty years next to him, believing they were being chased by his murderers. "I then kept my eye in the rearview mirror and I could see that the lights were there and that they were actually gaining on us as we proceeded down this highway," said Brown. Brown lost control of the car at the intersection of Highway 72 and Highway 172 and the vehicle came to rest in a ditch by the railroad track.

"We felt helpless, at least I did," said Brown, who shouted at a passing car, "Help us if you can, someone has been killed." The driver of the car summoned Colbert policeman Billy Smith, who then contacted Madison County sheriff Dewey Seagraves. The news of the murder would quickly reach President Lyndon Johnson.

A Klan Case

In his 1981 book *Murder at Broad River Bridge*, well-known Georgia political commentator Bill Shipp detailed the pattern of violence and destruction by the Ku Klux Klan in the Athens area in the early 1960s, such as the burning of a Catholic children's camp, which welcomed black youth, or the shooting of two black teenagers from cars owned by members of the Klan. There was also a group of KKK "nightriders" who drove the streets of Athens on "security patrol" with an emphasis on keeping the races apart. Jim Hudson, who along with John Darsey represented Myers and Sims in the murder trial and who died in 2010, said in a 2004 interview with this newspaper that there was never any question about the defendants' membership in the Klan.

"These fellows were members of the Ku Klux," said Hudson of his clients. "There wasn't any question about that; they didn't wear masks or anything. They were bona fide in their belief that the races ought not be integrated, which is wrong, but that's what they felt at the time. A lot of other people did too. Of course, it was wrong, still is."

When federal investigators came to Athens to investigate the Penn murder, they focused on the Klan, a group known to resort to violence to maintain segregation.

A Confession

The federal investigators began receiving tips from paid informants in the Klan. And one of the names that they kept hearing was James Lackey. So the agents began questioning Lackey, who first told them that he didn't know anything about the murder of Lemuel Penn and neither did Howard Sims nor Cecil Myers—a denial that was an unintended implication.

The FBI agents continued questioning Lackey, emphasizing that there would be no reward for speaking up except a clean conscience. And on August 6, Lackey confessed that he had driven the car in the shooting and that Sims and Myers were the gunmen. "I'm going to tell you the truth," Lackey told the FBI agents. "I drove the car. But I didn't think those sonofabitches were going to kill him."

He added, "When I was alongside the Negroes' car, both Myers and Sims fired shotguns into the Negroes' car. I drove on by the Negro car and turned around and came back. I didn't see the car into which the shots were fired as we returned from the area of the bridge to Athens."

Lackey's confession statement included several details about the night. For instance, he said Sims saw the D.C. tag of the car the victim was driving and commented, "That must be some of President Johnson's boys."

"The original reason for our following the colored men was because we had heard that Martin Luther King might make Georgia a testing ground with the Civil Rights Bill," said Lackey.

"We thought some out-of-town niggers might stir up some trouble in Athens." Lackey said Sims and Myers insisted that Lackey follow the car driven by the black men out of town. "They had me go out of town so it would not look like someone from Athens did the shooting," said Lackey.

Lackey said the gun used by Myers "was the shotgun that hangs on the wall of Guest's Garage" and that the gun used by Myers was "his own gun which he placed in the Chevy II earlier in the evening."

"As soon as we got back to Guest's Garage, both Myers and Sims cleaned the shotguns in the garage," Lackey said. "They wiped the guns off with a rag."

(Herbert) Guest asked what happened and Sims said, "We shot one, but we don't know if we killed him or not." Hudson contended that Lackey's confession was weak, and thus, so was the prosecution's case. "First of all, the only real evidence they had about us being involved was from [Lackey] the third guy driving the car," said Hudson in 2004.

"And Lackey had been so obviously coerced to testify. 'Cause he was a little bitty small guy and he was extremely nervous . . . If it's true, that he was the guy that was driving the car, then he was having to testify to something that he had done bad, and that in itself would lead me to believe that there was great coercion there." Federal agent James Simpson said Lackey's confession was a way to ease the burden of a guilty conscience.

"James Lackey's motive in confessing was not that he had been made promises, but rather was from relief from guilt," said Simpson, as quoted in Shipp's book. "Basically, Lackey seemed like a decent person who got caught up in something because he wanted to be part of a gang." Federal agents also questioned Herbert Guest, a garage owner and Klansman, who said that Sims and Myers told him they had killed Penn.

"[On July 12] Cecil Myers and Sims were talking in front of my garage," Guest told investigators. "I overheard one of them say that they thought the car had gone into the river and missed the bridge as they had not seen it all the way back to Athens. On Monday night, July 13, sometime after dark, I heard Sims and Cecil Myers's conversation at my garage. While I listened, they talked about the murder of Penn. Now, they told me they were the ones that shot at the car in which Penn was killed."

By the time the trial of Myers and Sims began, Lackey had spent several weeks in jail for his role in the murder and he issued another statement, recanting his previous implication of his two Klan friends as the gunmen.

A Denial of Charges

"After harassment for a period of thirty days with the loss of sleep and continued interrogation, after this my mental condition was at its lowest ebb and [I] was only glad to make any statements or sign anything," said Lackey, who refused to testify in the trial. Guest also refused to take the stand. But after much debate, statements from Lackey and Guest to investigators were admitted into court.

Meanwhile, Judge Skelton allowed Sims and Myers to take the stand without being cross-examined, and both testified that they had nothing to do with the killing. (The unsworn statement law was later ruled unconstitutional.) "I can assure you that I had nothing to do with this killing of Lemuel Penn," said Myers. "I believe that it is said that it happened about five o'clock in the morning, and I do believe that I was in town, in Athens now."

Hudson said he "didn't feel one way or another about it—their guilt or innocence," saying that a defense attorney can't worry about that. "I never do; I can't," said Hudson. "You just have to go on and do it."

"They never told me they did it and nobody ever confessed that they did it or none of the other people in the Ku Klux. They were just old working boys around town and surrounding counties, but nobody ever told me who did it. I didn't care."

Prosecution's Closing Arguments

Solicitor General Clete Johnson told jurors that statements from Lackey and Guest provided overwhelming evidence that Lackey had driven Myers and Sims and that the two gunmen committed cold-blooded murder. "These three men deliberately followed that car down that road for the purpose of indiscriminate murder," said Johnson. "They didn't care who they were killing . . . This killing was all unprovoked and there were no mitigating circumstances. It was just cold-blooded assassination." Johnson linked the killing to the assassination of John F. Kennedy just months earlier. "The assassination in this case, when they shot Lemuel A. Penn with a shotgun, it was just as great an assassination and just as much an assassination as when President Kennedy was shot down by a rifle, the same situation exactly . . ."

Johnson demanded that the jury recognize that no one had the right to take Lemuel Penn's life. "I submit to you that Lt. Col. Lemuel A. Penn was a man," said Johnson. "He could feel pain. He wanted to live. He thought as much of his life as these defendants think of theirs. He thought as much of his life as you do.

"He thought as much of his life as I do mine, and he had the right to live. Gentlemen, have the courage to do what's right." The prosecutor added that Madison County residents should be outraged that men from Athens brought their violent ways into the county.

"Let it be known to the world that Madison County don't appreciate people from Athens, Georgia, coming here . . . to kill people," said Johnson. "Let the world know that it's not right." The prosecutor called for the death penalty, saying that capital punishment was designed for cases in which "the crime is so revolting that the criminal responsible for it is not entitled to one parcel of sympathy or mercy, because they showed no sympathy or mercy."

"How can we show sympathy or mercy to people like this?" asked Johnson. "Now, gentlemen, this is a case where that extreme penalty is called for under the law to fit the circumstances." Clete Johnson's son, Don Johnson, was sixteen at the time of the trial.

He spoke at a 2006 sign dedication ceremony for Lemuel Penn. "It was a lot like a *To Kill a Mockingbird* scene," said Johnson. " It was still segregated, with the blacks in the balcony and everybody else downstairs. It was completely packed. There were news people from all over the world. It was as hot as it could be. There was no air conditioning. And I-85 was not completed. So Highway 29 was the main highway running south."

"So trucks ran around the courthouse and they had to shift down and shift up to get around the courthouse. So the judge made them detour around it because it was so loud with the windows open. It was a very interesting environment there."

Defense Team's Closing Arguments

Hudson argued that the prosecution's case was based on circumstantial evidence and that Lackey's confession was coerced. He reminded jurors of the testimony of a psychiatrist who said Lackey was mentally ill, "a man with a paranoid personality who doesn't trust anybody in the world."

"He thinks he has a misshapen head and thinks people stare at him and laugh," said Hudson, as quoted in Shipp's book.

And he has completely repudiated everything he said in the statement. While Hudson focused on Lackey, defense attorney John Darsey spoke out against the federal government, saying that FBI agents had been sent to Madison County with the instructions of "Don't come back until you bring us white meat." Shipp recalled in his book that Darsey "roared at the carpet bagging administration of justice," with President Johnson sending "swarms" of FBI agents to the area and "infiltrating our land."

"Never let it be said," Darsey shouted, "that a Madison County jury converted an electric chair into a sacrificial altar on which the pure flesh of a member of the human race was sacrificed to the savage, revengeful appetites of a raging mob . . . . When they couldn't get white meat, they built a sham of a case."

The Verdict

The jury suspended deliberations at 6:40 p.m., September 4, 1964, then resumed deliberations after dinner at 8:40 p.m. and reached a verdict at 10 p.m. "The courtroom was crowded and hot and absolutely silent," Shipp wrote.

"Mr. Foreman and gentlemen of the jury, have you reached a verdict?" Judge Skelton asked.

Henry Snelling, the clerk of court, read the verdict. "We, the jury, find the defendants, Joseph Howard Sims and Cecil Myers, not guilty." According to Shipp, there was applause and some cheering. And prosecutor Johnson even congratulated Sims and Myers. "There was nothing personal in this," he said.

Federal Convictions

In June 1966, nearly two years after the acquittal, Sims and Myers faced federal charges that they were part of a Klan conspiracy to keep out-of-state blacks out of the north Georgia area, using violence and intimidation to accomplish that aim. The two were tried in federal court in Athens. Hudson recalled that one day during the trial a photographer tried to snap a picture of Myers on the courthouse steps and the defendant knocked him down.

Hudson remembered that someone shouted, "G@#D@#$ Cecil, I don't believe I would have done that!" US attorney Floyd Buford prosecuted the Klansmen. "We are not trying Myers and Sims for murder," said Buford, as quoted by Shipp.

"We are trying them for conspiracy. But to prove our conspiracy charge, we are going to prove to you that [Penn's murder] was part of that plan . . . It was part of a broad conspiracy to keep out-of-state Negroes from coming into the Athens area." Both Sims and Myers were convicted on federal charges. Lackey, the driver of the car, never served a day in prison.

Fate of the Defendants

In May 1966, as he awaited the federal trial, Sims shot his thirty-five-year-old wife in the face, wounding, but not killing her. So Sims went to state prison for shooting his wife before serving his federal sentence, which began December 31, 1970, at the federal penitentiary in Terre Haute, Indiana. He was later transferred to Atlanta and released October 20, 1976.

At fifty-eight, Sims was shot once in the chest and killed by a twelve-gauge shotgun, the kind of gun used in the Penn murder, at a flea market. His killer was identified as his friend Edward U. Skinner. Myers served about six years from 1966 to 1972, first at Terre Haute and then at a minimum-security prison at Eglin Air Force Base, Florida.

He was released from all federal supervision on December 19, 1975. According to Shipp, Myers returned to northeast Georgia and worked as a truck driver, textile machinist, and brick mason. When the *Journal* tried to contact Myers by phone in 2004 for a story on the fortieth anniversary of the murder, a woman answered.

She said he was sleeping and could not talk, then she asked who's calling. When told that the newspaper was doing a piece on the Lemuel Penn murder and would like to speak with Cecil Myers, she responded, "He's not interested," and hung up.

Legacy of the Case

The Lemuel Penn murder case was nationally significant, a signature event in the Civil Rights era. Defense attorney Hudson said in 2004 that when he looked back on the Penn case and he thought that "tragic things are triggers to improvement."

"I'm not a particularly religious person, but a few years ago I was listening to this country preacher at a funeral," said Hudson. "He said this: 'God is so very kind that he will not let us hurt unless it is best.'

"And I've wondered about that, and thought about it for a couple of years. And I believe that was a true statement. Tragedy and everything else that happens to us: death, disability, all of those things eventually end up doing something good. So that's really the way I feel about the whole thing."

Shipp looked back on the case and remembered that "the slaying of Lemuel Penn was one the most tragic yet least noted acts of violence during the Civil Rights era."

"Penn was slain for no reason other than he happened to be black and his car bore D.C. license plates," wrote Shipp in a 2004 interview with this newspaper.

"He was not a Civil-Rights activist and even sought to avoid confrontations during his sojourn in Georgia. Since he was not connected with the Movement, his death was all but shrugged off by many so-called Civil Rights leaders. Penn was simply serving his country as a military reserve officer when he came to Georgia and lost his life."

He added, "Fortunately, our state leaders reacted swiftly and properly to investigate the murder and demonstrate to the nation that we would not tolerate such outrages. Georgia was spared much of the turmoil that other Southern states suffered during the 1960s simply because our leaders made it clear that they would not abide lawlessness in the name of defying the federal government." Shipp also noted that "Madison County bears no special responsibility for Col. Penn's death."

"What happened to Penn in Madison County could have happened in 1964 to him or someone like him in almost any other rural county in the South," said Shipp. "He was an innocent and random victim of hate in a regional revolution that could have been much more devastating."

Penn's Daughter Talks About Learning of the Murder

Linda Yancey, Lemuel Penn's oldest daughter, was asked in 2004 if she would be willing to share any of her memories of her father or if she might give some perspective on how the family responded to the murder. She responded with this written account:

On the night of July 10, 1964, our father had called, as usual to speak with each of us—my mother, brother, sister, and myself—but to go over his itinerary for his return trip to our home in Washington, D.C. from Army Reserve Training at Fort Benning in the state of Georgia.

In preparation, my sister, Sharon, and I had made new dresses. My mother, Georgia, had made a concerted effort to make special preparations for our father since they had not seen each other in two weeks. We were all concerned due to the warning given by those in command at the military installation of imminent Ku Klux Klan (Caucasians who wore white robes with two eye-hole openings in hoods, equipped with ropes for hanging, crosses for burning, as a means for frightening and controlling the Negro population or anyone else who believed in equality for all) activity in the area surrounding the Army Post of Ft. Benning.

Early on the morning of July 11, 1964, our mother, Georgia Penn, received the most heartbreaking information from Charles E. Brown, one of the other two reservists returning to the Washington Metropolitan area, that her beloved companion had been in an accident on Hwy. 172 outside of Colbert, Georgia. This man, a humanitarian, who would always assist others because he saw them as human beings—not for their ethnicity, color, or creed—had been assassinated unmercifully by a passing carload of Caucasians firing two shotgun blasts into the car containing Lemuel Penn, the driver and the two other reservists, Charles E. Brown and John Howard.

At this moment, Georgia calmly went to the rooms of her three children: Linda, age 14; Sharon, age 11; and Lem, Jr., age 4; to awaken them. Another telephone call would be received with more details—that her beloved had been assassinated. Meanwhile, my sister and I were bathing in our bathroom and were only able to hear bits and pieces of the telephone conversation. Hearing, the word "accident" sounded ridiculous, since our dad had never had one. Eventually, our mother would have each of us meet in my bedroom, to quietly tell us that our wonderful, loving father had been in an automobile accident—that he had been shot. Immediately, I inquired several times as to whether he was alive. Finally, she responded that our father had entered another world. (Imagine how she must have felt—here was a man who had served meritoriously in World War II in the Philippines, returning without one scratch, to be wounded fatally during a time of peace—what was she going to do without her beloved companion since they were still very much in love? How would she raise the children, although she knew there were sufficient finances, but her husband had always handled these? What was she going to do?)

Somehow, the neighbors were alerted. Fortunately, three or four physicians, an attorney, an opera singer and three educators resided on our street who were family friends. The physician across the street came over as soon as he heard. Somehow, our home environment was still, like the early morn. Family members, very close friends, and the like began appearing/calling to express their deepest sympathy and assisting with the multitudinous arrangements for the return of our father's remains. My mother also had the task of informing our father's mother and sister of his demise. Where were we, what were we doing at this time? We, the children were kept busy with our normal activities for a while, such as straightening our bedrooms, eating breakfast, taking care of our tri-colored collie, Zorro, etc.

Our mother allowed my brother to ride his red tricycle outside on the front sidewalk for a few moments. After a fashion, I had him come inside since he was saying, "My Dad has been shot," repeatedly as he rode back and forth in front of the house. The first and second levels of our home were maintained in a normal state. Towards the latter part of the morning, family members began organizing everything in the recreation room located in the basement of our home. In due time, reporters, curious bypassers—whether in cars or on foot—would begin appearing on our street for the next few days. The telephone rang constantly. The military sent a special escort to notify my mother of dad's demise along with making arrangements for his return, etc. We went to the airport one dark, rainy night to meet the airplane returning our father's body in a flag-draped casket with a special military honor guard.

At this point, the funeral director had arrived with his hearse, to prepare the body of Lt. Col. Lemuel A. Penn for the customary period of mourning (the wake—viewing of the body by family, friends, associates for two to three days), the church service conducted by Reverend Stanford Harris at the Asbury Methodist Church. When the funeral cortege arrived at the gates of Arlington National Cemetery, the casket was trans-ferred to the same caisson used for President John F. Kennedy with the same white horses. The pathway to his burial site all through the cemetery was lined with men in uniform of all branches of the service saluting as the caisson passed by. In other words, full military honors, including the 21-gun salute to his final resting place in Arlington National Cemetery in Arlington, Va. (July 20, 1964).

Our beloved mother decided to take a year of sabbatical leave from her positon as a home economics instructor on the middle school level to provide love and support for us, her three children. She succumbed from grief and lupus.

Georgia and Lemuel Penn had not only provided their children with a wealth of experiences at a very early age, but had also instilled a very high set of standards to last them a lifetime. Their legacy was carried on because all three children completed their education at institutions of higher learning becoming successful in their fields—Linda, an educator for 32 years; Sharon, an insurance litigator, Lemuel Jr., a captain with a major airline. All three children have married. Lemuel has two sons and Linda has a daughter who followed in her grandfather's stead. She is a graduate of the United States Naval Academy and is serving her second tour of duty in the Middle East.

—Linda Yancey,
daughter of Lemuel A. Penn

About the Author

Dr. Nathaniel J. Fuller is a technical architect with extensive background in designing and evaluating network and software applications/prototypes; in teaching undergraduate and graduate students principles in computer security; in cryptography and security mechanisms; in advanced network security; in networking concepts and applications; in system analysis, planning, and control; in principles of information security and privacy; in web security; in wireless communication systems; in database concepts; in network security; and in enterprise network management.

As a former computer scientist for the United States (US) Federal Government, Dr. Fuller has led and supported several cyber software and network development efforts and has received multiple technology awards.

As a former avionic technician (AT) for the US Navy, he supervised and performed technical maintenance on communications, radar, navigation, data link, fire control, and tactical displays for numerous naval aircraft.

Dr. Fuller has a doctorate degree in computer information systems (CIS) and masters in CIS from Nova Southeastern University (NSU), masters in aeronautical science and bachelor of science in management of technical operations from Embry-Riddle Aeronautical University (ERAU), and bachelor of science in CIS from Saint Leo University.